CREOLE
flavors

CREOLE
flavors

*Recipes for Marinades,
Rubs, Sauces, and Spices*

KEVIN GRAHAM

Photographs by
ZEVA OELBAUM

ARTISAN • NEW YORK

Published in 1996 by
ARTISAN
a division of Workman Publishing Company, Inc.
708 Broadway, New York, New York 10003

LIBRARY OF CONGRESS
CATALOGING-IN-PUBLICATION DATA

Graham, Kevin.
    Creole flavors: recipes for marinades, rubs, sauces, and
spices / Kevin Graham: photographs by Zeva Oelbaum.
        p.   cm.
    Includes index.
    ISBN 1-885183-22-4
    1. Condiments. 2. Marinades. 3. Sauces. 4. Cookery, Creole.
5. Cookery, American—Louisiana style.
    TX819.AIG73   1996
    641.6 382—dc20   95-49377

PRINTED IN ITALY

10   9   8   7   6   5   4   3   2   1

first printing

To *the memory of* Tilly

CONTENTS

THERE IS AN OLD ADAGE, "adopt, adapt, and improve." This saying certainly applies to Creole cuisine, for rather than being truly indigenous, it is a representation of all of the different cultures that have left their mark on New Orleans, from French to Spanish to African. Visitors flock year-round to the fine restaurants and more casual dining establishments of New Orleans, to sample such delicious dishes as Jambalaya and Seafood Gumbo and to revel in the Creole love of entertaining and general *joie de vivre*.

EATING IS A CRUCIAL PART OF LIFE in New Orleans, and mealtime continues to be the focal point of the day. In fact, it is not uncommon for locals to sit down to the table for a noontime meal and stay there, eating, drinking wine, and convivially conversing until the evening meal, all the while helping themselves to seconds, then dessert, coffee, and liqueurs or cognac. This is a very French practice, but then Louisiana was first and foremost a French colony. Established in 1718 on the high ground adjacent to the Mississippi River, it became Spanish for a time (1764–1800), and it is actually Spanish architecture we see in the old French Quarter of New Orleans, with its lacy wrought-iron balconies and brick courtyards with fountains and lush greenery. Very briefly

French again (1800–1803), Louisiana became an American territory in 1803 as part of the Louisiana Purchase.

THE RESIDENTS WHO SETTLED in the area during these various governments influenced the local culinary heritage, gradually blending their respective cooking and eating styles into a distinct local Creole cuisine, all the while using indigenous ingredients, including rice, game, local fruits and vegetables, and a year-round supply of fresh seafood from the Gulf of Mexico and Lake Pontchartrain, as well as ingredients from other places that were regularly transported through the vital New Orleans port: fine wines from France, spices from the Far East, rum from the Caribbean, and exotic produce and fruit from far and near.

TO THESE INFLUENCES, add the significance of the Africans who, as cooks and housekeepers in the homes of the wealthy as well as the merchant middle class well into the twentieth century, contributed a touch of African tradition and reinterpreted French dishes. For instance, the Gumbo (page 128) so greatly loved locally is named for the gelatinous vegetable okra usually used to thicken it; "gumbo" means okra in an African dialect, and the plant's seeds were brought to this country hidden in the hair of the slaves. Moreover, perhaps due to a French heritage and an inherent laissez-faire attitude, even before the Civil War the city of New Orleans had a sizable community of free blacks who were allowed to own property and operate businesses.

WHEN NON-LOUISIANANS think of the food of this region, they commonly lump it all under the Cajun moniker, or call Cajun food Creole. The two cultures are actually very distinct. The Cajuns are descended from the Frenchmen driven from Acadia when the Canadian territory was ceded to the English in 1713 and renamed Nova Scotia. These French loyalists gradually made their way south to the new French territory and settled happily in southern Louisiana, where they made their way as before, as hunters, trappers, and fishermen, along the verdant waterways they called bayous. Gradually in their French patois, derived from old French, Acadian became Cajun, and this word came to describe their dialect and all aspects of their lifestyle, including their music and food.

THESE COUNTRY PEOPLE were quite different from the more commercially minded, city-dwelling Creoles, and their Cajun cuisine reflects this. While based on the same French techniques and fresh ingredients, Cajun is much heartier and simpler fare, incorporating many bayou ingredients, such as rabbit, alligator, and raccoon, into slow-cooked stews. It is also much spicier, as everyone knows from the national food trend of the mid- to late-1980s.

NEW ORLEANS' CREOLE COOKING, however, is not very different from the *haute cuisine* espoused by Auguste Escoffier in Europe more than one hundred years ago. The first French settlers in New Orleans adopted the classical European way of doing things, from raising their own produce to cooking and entertaining, but adapted these methods to the local products.

MANY OF THE CREOLE DISHES we see on tables in New Orleans today can easily be traced to the dishes from which they were derived. For instance, the traditional Lobster Bisque of France became in New Orleans Crawfish Bisque, and the Jambalaya (page 24) we eat today is essentially Spanish Paella with a Creole twist. Or simply look in this book to the local interpretations of Mayonnaise (page 124), Rémoulade Sauce (pages 58 and 59), Cocktail Sauce (pages 63 and 64), and spice blends or marinades, all similar to yet distinctively evolved from the original products. For instance, Creole Mustard (page 57) is a more fiery version of the similar whole-grain mustard still made in Dijon, France. Professional chefs and housewives in New Orleans continue to cook with French roux, with which they build, thicken, and color a dish, such as Seafood Gumbo, Crawfish Etouffé, or Shrimp Creole. And Creole cooks use the same techniques for making and incorporating rich stocks that have been used by French cooks for centuries.

WHILE WORKING ON THIS BOOK, my research took me back to the Creole cook of yesteryear, whether she be the lady of the house or the servant. I studied what was necessary to set a traditional table and what stores I needed in my pantry to achieve this. As we now have modern appliances and techniques to simplify the job at hand, I, in turn, simplified and reinterpreted classic Creole recipes, bringing them into the twentieth century for the cooks of today.

ABOVE ALL, THE CREOLE home cook was a practical person. From her European ancestors she inherited frugality, yet was not stingy in her ways. Everything was used and nothing went to waste. In my recipe for Homemade Sweet Butter (page 120), I suggest using the leftover buttermilk in other dishes; and Hog's Head Cheese (page 116) is a dish originally made with the head and feet left over from an animal slaughtered in the fall. This recipe and the Duck Confit (page 54) would have lasted months, needing no refrigeration when put up properly in jars or earthenware crocks; they are prepared in the same way that the French make their *rillettes* and *confits*. Our Creole lady of the house would make Lavender Sachets (page 34) from her garden to repel moths and keep linen fresh during the long, hot summers. Or she would flavor liqueurs and spirits with blossoms (see Orange Blossom Liqueur on page 76) or fruit (see Kumquat-Flavored Rum on page 79) to enliven other dishes or to serve guests after a fine meal.

THE CREOLE COOK WAS limited only by her imagination and the diversity of her garden or the marketplace. South Louisiana's tropical climate and rich, alluvial soil enriched by eons of river flooding allowed Creole homes and plantation gardens to prosper with fresh herbs, vegetables, fruit trees, and glorious flowering plants. In days gone by, pickling was a simple but effective way of preserving summer's bounty, for even Louisiana endures winter, though it is generally mild. For me, nothing brightens a winter table like a large bowl of Green Tomato Relish (page 108) or Sweet Corn Relish (page 106). And who can resist homemade Pontchatoula Strawberry Jam (page 46), a taste of summer on a bleak January morning?

THERE ARE MANY POINTS to remember when putting up foods, whether they are pickled, jellied, or a jam or relish. The old pantries didn't have windows, as the Creoles realized that the biggest food spoiler was light. Keep in mind when putting up your supplies of homemade items that they will keep better and longer in a cool, dry place away from all light sources, such as at the back of a cabinet or an infrequently used closet.

INTERESTINGLY, HOME CANNERS owe a debt of thanks to the French Emperor Napoleon II. Knowing that any army marches on its stomach, Napoleon Bonaparte offered 12,000 francs to anyone who could find a way to preserve food to feed his armies as they marched across Europe. In 1809 François Appert, a Parisian confectioner, devised a way to preserve food in glass containers that were processed in a hot water bath, and it is this method that we still use today. Perhaps, then, it is only fitting that the French-descended Creoles were so proficient at canning and preserving the summer harvest for enjoying later in the year. Specific instructions for sterilizing jars and processing in a water bath are given on pages 134 and 135.

A COMMON TERM in Creole parlance is "lagniappe," meaning "a little something extra." This gracious practice is prevalent among restaurateurs and food merchants in New Orleans, sometimes used as a commercial enticement but more often to thank customers for their patronage. Whether lagniappe takes the form of an extra oyster or two shucked with the standard dozen, a particularly generous helping on a Po' Boy Sandwich, complimentary coffee, or fresh tomatoes along with the regular order from the greengrocer, this carry-over from a bygone era is both quaint and heartwarming, ensuring loyalty for the merchant and satisfaction for the customer.

IN MANY WAYS lagniappe summarizes a Creole custom perpetuated in all manner of everyday life. It is a demonstration of sharing, a part of the overall love of life held dear to the Creole heart. As a relative newcomer to the very special city of New Orleans, I have been the grateful recipient of much lagniappe. And with this book I hope to share much of what I have received.

RES, RUBS
& marinades

THE USES FOR CREOLE SEASONING are as infinite as the ingredients you use in your cooking. For meats, rub the seasoning into the flesh from 1 hour to 24 hours before sautéing or grilling. Sprinkle the seasoning over vegetables before grilling or stir-frying. Or, for a simple pasta dish, dice half of a large yellow onion and sauté in 1 tablespoon olive oil. Add 1 teaspoon Creole Seasoning and cook for 1 minute. Toss with 2 cups hot cooked pasta, and voilà, dinner for two in a flash!

2 tablespoons freshly ground black pepper
2 tablespoons ground white pepper
2 tablespoons paprika
1 tablespoon powdered sugar
1 tablespoon salt
1 tablespoon garlic powder
2 teaspoons dried oregano
1 teaspoon ground thyme
1 teaspoon cayenne pepper
½ teaspoon ground celery seeds

Combine all of the ingredients in a mixing bowl, stirring well to incorporate. Store in an airtight container until ready to use.

Makes ½ cup

preceding pages: Citrus Salt

THESE TRIANGLES ARE A SIMPLE VARIATION of the more traditional cheese straws, which are made with cheddar cheese and shaped with either a cookie gun or by cutting by hand. I think you'll find that these are just as delicious and not as time-consuming to make. Serve them hot as an hors d'oeuvre or as an accompaniment to cream soups or seafood bisques. While these can be made up to one week ahead, they should not be frozen as the cheese will separate from the pastry.

½ package frozen puff pastry (1 sheet), thawed
½ cup grated Romano cheese
¼ cup grated Parmesan cheese
½ teaspoon freshly ground black pepper
2 teaspoons Creole Seasoning (opposite)
1 egg
½ cup milk

Unfold the sheet of pastry on a lightly floured surface. Roll the pastry into a 14-by-12-inch rectangle, about ¼ inch thick. Cover with a dry kitchen towel and allow to rest 30 minutes.

Combine the Romano and Parmesan cheeses and the spices in a mixing bowl. In a separate bowl, beat the egg with the milk to form a wash.

Lightly paint the puff pastry with the egg wash, then sprinkle with the cheese mixture, making sure the puff pastry is evenly coated. Gently press the cheese mixture onto the puff pastry so it will stay in place.

Preheat the oven to 325°F.

With a sharp knife, cut the pastry sheet in half lengthwise to form two 14-by-6-inch strips. Cut vertically at 1-inch increments along both strips to form 28 1-by-6-inch strips, then cut each strip in half diagonally to form 56 triangles. Carefully remove the triangles and place on a baking sheet. Bake the triangles in the preheated oven until the cheese is golden brown, about 20 minutes.

Remove the triangles from the oven and allow to cool slightly on wire racks before serving. Serve immediately or store in an airtight container at room temperature for up to 1 week.

Makes 4½ dozen

I THINK YOU'LL BE DELIGHTED not only by the delicate tartness of home-made cheese, but also by how simple it is to make. Crumble this Creole Cheese into salads or serve as a snack with crackers or sliced fresh bread. You can also cook with Creole Cheese as you would Ricotta. If desired, adjust the seasoning by adding fresh herbs or a little freshly sliced truffle, if you can afford it! This cheese will keep for 1 to 2 weeks in the refrigerator and during that time the flavors will intensify.

Note that this recipe must be made with whole milk; skim and low-fat milk are too watery. The amount of time you press the cheese when refrigerated determines its final consistency. For creamier cheese with a higher fat content, press it for less time, about 4 hours. For a denser cheese, press it longer, about 12 hours.

½ gallon whole milk
¼ cup freshly squeezed lemon juice
1 teaspoon Creole Seasoning (page 18)
¼ teaspoon salt
2 cloves garlic, peeled and minced
Freshly ground black pepper to taste

Place the milk in a deep, heavy saucepan over high heat. Bring the milk almost to a boil, stirring frequently to prevent it from burning on the sides and bottom of the pan. Remove the pan from the heat and slowly stir in the lemon juice. The milk will begin to curdle and turn a greenish color. Cover the pan and allow to sit for 15 minutes at room temperature.

Line a sieve or colander with 3 layers of cheesecloth and pour the curdled milk through. Drain the milk for 10 to 15 minutes. Gently fold the Creole Seasoning, salt, and garlic into the curds. Gather the edges of the cheesecloth like a bag and tie the top tightly with string. Hang the cheese bundle over a bowl for 1 hour, or until the curds are completely drained and firm.

Place the cheesecloth bag in a bowl or mold just large enough to hold it tightly. Cover with a plate topped with a 1-pound weight or a container holding 10 cups water. Refrigerate the cheese for at least 8 hours, or until it reaches the desired consistency (longer for a denser cheese, less for a creamier cheese).

When the cheese is firm, remove it from the refrigerator and discard any liquid that may have settled underneath. Unmold the cheese and peel away the cheesecloth. Sprinkle the outside of the cheese with freshly ground black pepper and serve with crackers or use in other dishes.

Makes ¾ to 1 quart

USE CREOLE HERBS in soups, stocks, or vinaigrettes. This versatile herb mixture is obviously related to the French Herbes de Provence.

¼ cup dried thyme
¼ cup dried marjoram
¼ cup dried savory
5 medium bay leaves, crushed
2 tablespoons dried oregano leaves
1 tablespoon dried rosemary
1 teaspoon dried lavender blossoms (page 34)
1 teaspoon powdered sage
1 teaspoon dried tarragon
1 teaspoon red pepper flakes

Combine all of the ingredients in a mixing bowl and stir well to combine. Store in an airtight container indefinitely.

Makes 1 cup

RUB THIS DELICIOUS MARINADE on steak, chicken, or leg of lamb (my favorite) before grilling. Also try tossing it with cut potatoes before roasting. Use 1 tablespoon marinade per 8 ounces meat or potatoes.

> *2 teaspoons Creole Herbs (opposite)*
> *1 teaspoon salt*
> *1 teaspoon freshly ground black pepper*
> *2 tablespoons pure olive oil*
> *1 teaspoon minced garlic*

Combine all of the ingredients in a small bowl and rub into meat or poultry at least 8 to 24 hours before grilling.

Makes ¼ cup

CREOLE *marinade*

JAMBALAYA

I BELIEVE THE SPANISH brought paella to New Orleans and over time it became jambalaya. There are simply too many similarities between the two dishes for this theory to be dismissed as mere coincidence. Whatever its name, this spicy rice dish lends itself to all varieties of fish, meat, or fowl.

When making seafood jambalaya, I suggest you use chicken (not fish) stock and leave the shells on the shrimp to give the dish added flavor. Also, add the seafood only during the last 10 minutes of cooking to keep it from drying out and becoming tough. Instead of using just chicken or seafood, try any combination of ingredients to suit your taste.

While in France andouille is made with tripe, garlic, and spices, in southeastern Louisiana andouille is a spicy pork sausage. This leads some people to believe that the andouille of Louisiana, though French in name, is of German origin. Louisiana was, in fact, host to a large community of German immigrants in the last century. A good example is the southeastern town of Des Allemands (translated from the French to "The Germans"), catfish capital of the state.

By cooking the chicken and sausage in a little water as done here, I have eliminated the need for additional fats or oils in which to cook the meat. As the water evaporates it naturally renders the fat under the chicken skin and in the sausage, keeping the meat moist and leaving enough fat in which to cook the vegetables and rice. If you decide to use only seafood in your jambalaya instead of the chicken and andouille or a combination of the three, be sure to use ¼ cup vegetable oil when sautéing your vegetables.

While the final cooking of the Jambalaya can be done on the stove top, I prefer to place the pot in the oven as this ensures more even cooking and that the rice won't become gummy. To ensure your pot will fit inside your stove, invert the lid so the handle is inside! And don't stir the Jambalaya during the final cooking process, as this will make the rice clump.

1 2- to 3-pound chicken, skin on, or
   1 pound fresh seafood (shrimp, crawfish tails, or oysters)
   or any combination of ingredients
2 cups andouille sausage or other hot smoked sausage,
   cut into ¼-inch slices
2 large yellow onions, peeled and diced
1 large green bell pepper, cored, seeded, and diced
4 cloves garlic, peeled and chopped
1½ cups long-grain rice
2 teaspoons Creole Herbs (page 22)
½ teaspoon paprika
½ teaspoon cayenne pepper
2 bay leaves
1 clove
8 cups homemade Chicken Stock (page 132) or
   canned reduced-sodium chicken broth

Preheat the oven to 375°F.

Cut the chicken into 2-inch pieces, leaving the bone and skin intact. Place the chicken and sausage in a large, heavy stockpot with ½ cup water. Place the pot over medium-high heat and when the water has evaporated, brown the chicken and sausage in the rendered fat, stirring occasionally.

Add the onion, bell pepper, and garlic to the pot with the chicken and sausage. Sauté the vegetables over medium heat until the onions are translucent, about 2 minutes. Add the rice, Creole Herbs, and other seasonings to the pan and stir well. Add the chicken stock to the pan and bring to a boil over high heat.

Cover the pan and bake in the preheated oven until the stock has been absorbed, about 30 minutes. (Alternately, cook the mixture, covered, on the stove over medium heat.) Add seafood (if using) 10 minutes before the jambalaya is finished cooking.

Remove the pan from the oven, stir the jambalaya, and season with salt and pepper to taste. Serve immediately.

Serves 10 to 12

CITRUS salt

THIS IS BASICALLY A CURING SALT, although it makes an excellent addition to other foods. By pressing the citrus fruit into the salt, the fruit's oils are released, and the salt in turn imparts a light citrus essence into other foods. This seasoned salt is great for adding aromatic flavor to cured fish as well as vinaigrettes, and can also be used to season meat, poultry, and seafood.

> *1 box (26 ounces) salt*
> *4 lemons*
> *4 limes*
> *4 oranges*

Allow the fruit to come to room temperature. Spread the salt on a flat working surface and firmly roll 1 lemon at a time into the salt, pressing down hard with the palm of your hand to release the oils. Repeat with the remaining 3 lemons and the limes and oranges.

Discard the lemons, limes, and oranges, or wash and use for another recipe. Mix the salt well and store in airtight containers until ready to use.

Makes 3 ¼ cups

THIS IS A CREOLE VARIATION on court-bouillon, a classic poaching liquid used by the French to flavor seafood. The Creoles in Louisiana took this simple cooking staple, added their usual zest, and boiled seafood has never been the same! Try cooking freshly caught shrimp, crabs, and crawfish with Seafood Boil Mix. The recipe given here yields enough seasoning to flavor 5 pounds of seafood or vegetables in 2 gallons boiling water.

Seafood Boil Mix can also be used as a dry marinade: Simply grind it in a clean coffee grinder, then sprinkle on meats, seafood, or poultry before cooking. Or, use a bit of Seafood Boil Mix to flavor other foods, such as Pickled Okra (page 112).

1 4-inch square cheesecloth
4 cloves
2 crumbled bay leaves
2 tablespoons salt
1 tablespoon crushed white peppercorns
1 tablespoon crushed black peppercorns
1 tablespoon mustard seeds
1 teaspoon red pepper flakes
1 teaspoon ground allspice
1 teaspoon dried thyme
1 teaspoon celery seeds
Pinch nutmeg

Place the square of cheesecloth on a flat work surface and place all of the ingredients in the center. Gather up the cloth to form a bundle, twisting up the ends, and tie tightly with string. Place the bundle in boiling water to flavor seafood, meat, or vegetables.

Makes ⅓ cup

CRAWFISH boil

FOR A GREAT BACKYARD COOKOUT, try boiling seafood the way they do down in the bayou country in southern Louisiana.

3 large onions
3 heads garlic, unpeeled, cut across the diameter
3 bundles Seafood Boil Mix (page 27)
3 pounds fresh, shucked corn on the cob
3 pounds fresh red bliss potatoes, scrubbed
24 pounds fresh crawfish (see Note) or
   crabs, or 10 pounds shrimp (heads on)

Place 10 gallons water, the onions, garlic, and Seafood Boil bundles in a large, heavy stockpot, or divide between 2 stockpots. Bring the mixture to a boil over high heat. Lower the heat and simmer for 10 minutes before adding the corn and potatoes. Cook for 10 minutes, then add the seafood to the pot and return to a boil. Remove the pot from the heat, cover, and allow to stand 20 minutes. Carefully drain the seafood and vegetables into a large colander. Discard the cooking liquid, seafood bundles, onions, and garlic.

Spread newspapers on a table and serve the seafood and vegetables directly on the newspapers. Eat the seafood and vegetables as soon as they are cool enough to handle, or refrigerate for a cool supper. If desired, serve with Creole Rémoulade (page 59) or Creole Cocktail Sauce (page 63) for dipping.

NOTE: If you are boiling freshly caught crawfish, make sure you purge them before boiling, following the directions in the Crawfish Oil recipe (page 95); otherwise you will have a very muddy dish!

Serves 6

THIS MARINADE ADDS A DELICIOUS FLAVOR to meats. Lightly sprinkle the marinade on both sides of a steak and allow it to sit at room temperature for 3 hours before cooking. (During this time, the sugar and spices will dissolve and a percentage will be absorbed into the flesh, giving the meat an extraordinarily rich flavor.) Cook the steak to desired doneness, being careful not to cook it too quickly or over too high a high heat, as this will cause the sugar to burn and become bitter.

> *2 cups packed light brown sugar*
> *1 teaspoon red pepper flakes*
> *1 teaspoon Creole Herbs (page 22)*
> *1 teaspoon Citrus Salt (page 26)*
> *1 teaspoon paprika*

Combine all of the ingredients in a mixing bowl. Store in an airtight container at room temperature until ready to use. This marinade will keep indefinitely in an airtight container.

Makes 2 cups

SALT CURED FISH was probably brought to South Louisiana by the Spanish, and salt cod, or *bacalao*, is still served on local tables on Good Friday. Try serving cured fish as either an hors d'oeuvre with Creole Rémoulade (page 59) or French Rémoulade (page 58) and sliced French bread, or as a first course with fresh homemade Mayonnaise (page 124) or dilled sour cream and toast points. Fish cured in this manner will keep for up to 1 month in the refrigerator.

> *1 cup Citrus Salt (page 26)*
> *1 cup granulated sugar*
> *1 teaspoon crushed black peppercorns*
> *1 teaspoon crushed white peppercorns*
> *¼ teaspoon cayenne pepper*
> *2 2-pound boned fillets of firm, white fish,*
>   *such as grouper, red snapper, or redfish*

Line a shallow tray with a clean kitchen towel. Combine all of the dry ingredients in a bowl and mix well. Place 1 fish fillet, skin side down, on the kitchen towel in the tray. Rub all of the dry spice mixture into the flesh and cover with the other fish fillet, flesh side down. Cover the fish with a second clean kitchen towel and top with a flat dish. Place a 5-pound weight (or 10 cups of water in a deep dish) on top of the fish. Place the weighted fish in the refrigerator overnight.

Remove the fish from the refrigerator, remove the weights, and turn over the 2 fish fillets without separating. Rewrap the fish and replace the dish and weights. Return to the refrigerator for another 24 hours.

Remove the fish from the refrigerator, remove the weights, and unwrap the fish fillets. Wash the fish fillets quickly under cold running water for 2 minutes to remove the remaining spice mixture. Pat the fish dry and slice thinly on a cutting board. Place the fish slices on a decorative platter and serve.

Makes 4 pounds

QUATRE ÉPICES

THIS BLEND OF FOUR SPICES was traditionally used in home charcuterie, which flourished in southeast Louisiana during the last century and the first half of this one. Unfortunately, the tradition of hand-cut meats and home-cured meat products has gone out of fashion with the ease of one-stop supermarket shopping and because we are no longer allowed to keep pigs in our backyards (especially in Uptown New Orleans)!

Grind Quatre Épices in a clean coffee grinder, then store in an airtight container in the freezer. Be sure to use whole spices when making the blend, as preground spices lack flavor.

Rub 1 teaspoon of the ground spices into a pork roast 2 hours before cooking, add a pinch to candied yams, or serve them in mashed potatoes as an accompaniment to Hog's Head Cheese (page 116)—you'll be quite surprised by the intensity of flavors in this combination.

½ cup white peppercorns
2 tablespoons dried ginger
2 tablespoons freshly ground nutmeg
4 cloves

Combine all of the ingredients in a clean coffee grinder and blend for 1 minute. Store in an airtight container in the freezer until ready to use. Quatre Épices will keep indefinitely in the freezer.

Makes ½ cup

BRANDADE, A CURED FISH PURÉE, is a dish common to all European sea-faring nations. Because it was easy to store for long trips, it provided easy rations for maritime fleets.

Spread your Brandade on toasted French bread slices and serve as an hors d'oeuvre or use as a filling in an omelet. The Brandade will keep for 1 week in the refrigerator.

> *1½ pounds Cured Fish (page 31)*
> *1 medium potato, peeled, boiled, and quartered*
> *3 cloves garlic, peeled and crushed*
> *Pinch Quatre Épices (opposite)*
> *1 cup whole milk, at room temperature*
> *1 cup pure olive oil*
> *Juice of 1 lemon*

Place the fish in a large, heavy stockpot and cover with cold water. Bring to a boil over high heat, then remove from the heat and allow to cool. Remove the fish from the water and drain. Peel off the skin and discard, then break the flesh into pieces.

Place the fish, quartered potato, garlic, and Quatre Épices in a food processor and blend on low speed for 1 minute. Scrape the sides of the bowl with a spatula and blend again for 2 minutes, gradually adding the milk while the machine is running. Scrape the sides of the bowl and blend again, adding the olive oil and lemon juice.

Season to taste with salt and pepper. Pour the Brandade into a decorative bowl and serve.

Makes 2 pounds

LAVENDER sachets

IT'S QUITE SIMPLE to dry your own lavender. Simply tie a string around the fresh lavender stems to form a bundle and hang in a dark, dry place, such as a closet or attic, until the blossoms fall easily, about 2 weeks depending on the temperature.

Creole ladies in days gone by made these sachets to scent their armoires and repel moths. For a pretty effect, place a 6-inch square of lace around the cheesecloth before securing the sachet with ribbon.

When making Lavender Sachets, reserve a few teaspoons of the dried blossoms in an air-tight container and keep in the kitchen for making Lavender Ice Cream (opposite), adding to Creole Herbs (page 22), or imparting a subtle fragrance to other dishes.

> *4 6-inch cheesecloth squares*
> *1 cup dried lavender blossoms*
> *4 12-inch ribbons*

Place one cheesecloth square flat on a working surface. Into the center of the muslin cloth, place ¼ cup dried lavender blossoms. Gather up the cloth to form a bundle, twisting up the ends. Tie the bundle tightly with a ribbon to form a sachet. Repeat with the remaining cheesecloth squares, lavender, and ribbon.

Hang sachets in your closet to impart a lightly perfumed scent to your clothing.

Makes 4 Sachets

THE LAVENDER BLOSSOMS RELEASE a strong perfume, so only 1 teaspoon is needed to scent this unusual ice cream.

> *2 cups heavy cream*
> *2 cups milk*
> *¾ cup Vanilla Sugar (page 38) or granulated sugar*
> *1 teaspoon dried lavender blossoms (opposite)*
> *10 large egg yolks*

Combine the cream, milk, Vanilla Sugar, and lavender blossoms in a heavy saucepan over medium heat and bring to a boil. As soon as the mixture boils, remove the pan from the heat. Place the egg yolks in a large bowl and whisk to blend. Strain the hot milk mixture through a fine sieve into a clean pan and discard the lavender blossoms. Add the strained milk mixture to the yolks, a little at a time, whisking constantly.

When all of the milk mixture has been incorporated, strain again into a heavy saucepan and place over medium-low heat. Cook, stirring constantly with a wooden spoon, for about 10 minutes, or until the mixture is thick enough to coat the back of the spoon. Remove the pan from the heat and let cool to room temperature.

Pour the cream mixture into an ice cream maker and freeze according to the manufacturer's instructions. (Alternately, pour the mixture into a large shallow bowl and place in the freezer. Stir the mixture every 10 to 15 minutes until the ice cream has set.)

Makes 3 pints

overleaf: Lavender Ice Cream

VANILLA SUGAR CAN REPLACE granulated sugar in recipes calling for vanilla extract, such as ice creams or brulées, or it can be added to whipping cream when topping desserts. It also gives morning coffee a delicious, rich flavor.

Another interesting flavored sugar is orange sugar. Unfortunately, making it is a very tedious process and there are no shortcuts. One by one, gently grate sugar cubes against the skin of an orange; the abrasive texture of the sugar cube breaks the orange's tender surface, releasing the fruit's delicate oil into it. After you have the desired number of cubes, place them on a baking sheet and allow to dry for 3 days in a warm place, then crush them into a powder with a rolling pin. Use the flavored sugar to sweeten iced tea or, as with the Vanilla Sugar, in any dessert recipe. You can also make flavored sugar with lemons or limes.

I'm sure that making Vanilla Sugar was common practice in old Louisiana. I can't help but wonder if it may have been the first way syrups were made to flavor the crushed ice for our beloved summer "snowballs." In fact, the most famous of these snowball stands is on the street where I live, Plum Street.

10 cups granulated sugar
4 ounces (about 16 pods) whole Tahitian vanilla pods

Place the sugar in a large mixing bowl. With a sharp knife, split the vanilla beans down the middle to expose the small black seeds. With the back of a knife, scrape the tiny seeds from each pod and add them to the sugar. Chop the pods very finely, then mix into the sugar. Mix the sugar mixture with your hands to ensure the pods and seeds are evenly distributed. Cover the bowl with plastic wrap and allow to stand overnight.

Strain the sugar through a fine sieve to remove the chopped vanilla pods. Reserve the pods in an airtight container and refrigerate to be used again to flavor the same amount of sugar. Place the sugar in an airtight container and store at room temperature.

Makes 10 cups

Using Vanilla Sugar

THIS BASIC WHITE ICING can be used to decorate King Cake (recipe follows) or other cakes and rolls. It can be flavored with liqueurs, brandy or extracts, or colored with food coloring.

> *1½ cups Vanilla Sugar (opposite) or granulated sugar*
> *¼ cup water*
> *¾ cup light corn syrup*
> *Food coloring (optional)*

Place the sugar and water in a heavy saucepan and bring to a boil over medium heat, stirring until the sugar is dissolved. Add the corn syrup, stir well, and bring to a gentle boil. Brush the inside wall of the saucepan with water as the syrup cooks to prevent sugar crystals from forming. Cook the syrup until it reaches the soft ball stage or about 240°F. on a candy thermometer.

Remove the pan from the heat and pour the icing onto a cool platter. Work the fondant with a spoon or spatula until it comes together with no lumps and is firm and white, about 2 to 3 minutes. (At this point, the fondant can be placed in an airtight container and stored indefinitely in the refrigerator.)

To ice the King Cake, heat the fondant in the top of a double boiler over gentle heat, being careful not to heat above 95°F. as it will lose its shine and crystallize as it dries. (If desired, flavor the fondant with liqueurs or extracts while you are warming it up.) The fondant is ready when it runs off a spoon in a thick stream.

Divide the fondant icing among 3 small bowls and add 2 to 3 drops of food coloring to each bowl to make purple, green, and gold icing (mixing red and blue for purple). Add drops of water to thin the icing if it is too dry to spread smoothly.

Decorate the King Cake with alternating bands of different colors of icing. For added color while the icing is still soft, sprinkle with colored sugar or chopped nuts. (Colored sugar can be purchased or it can be made by combining food coloring and granulated sugar with an electric handmixer.)

Makes 2½ cups

KING CAKE

KING'S DAY FALLS ON JANUARY 6, Twelfth Night, or Epiphany, the date when the three wise men arrived in Bethlehem bearing gifts for the Christ Child. This is also the day when the Spanish traditionally celebrate Christmas, and hence the importance of this day in and around New Orleans, once a large Spanish stronghold. A popular custom to continue on this day is the baking of a special cake in honor of the three kings, and hence the King Cake.

The Creoles adopted the tradition of celebrating Twelfth Night, and it is on this night that Carnival actually begins, running through Mardi Gras, the day before Lent. (French for "Fat Tuesday," Mardi Gras is the day of merriment before the days of atonement during Lent.) Lavish balls are held throughout the Carnival season, and at each ball a king and queen are selected to reign over the festivities. Traditionally, two cakes were made—one for the ladies and one for the men—and a bean, a coin, or a golden bejeweled ring was placed in each one. The lucky guests who chose the pieces of cake with the surprises in them would then be king and queen for the evening.

This custom is still common throughout southeastern Louisiana at private parties, although at the larger balls the monarchs are now chosen long in advance by their social standing and prominence within their particular organization. Rather than a bean, coin, or ring, today commercial bakers place a plastic doll symbolic of baby Jesus in the cake. Home cooks should use a single dried bean, such as a kidney or lima bean, in their King Cakes.

King Cakes are similar to cinnamon rolls in flavor and texture and can be served either warm or at room temperature. King Cakes were originally made in a ring shape with little decoration, but they are now braided and trimmed in the traditional Mardi Gras colors suggested here (purple for justice, green representing faith, and gold for power or wealth). Decorate yours as you wish, adding pecan or walnut pieces to the dough or to the top; color the dough if desired.

> *4 cups all-purpose flour*
> *2 packages (4 ½ teaspoons) active dry yeast*
> *⅓ cup Vanilla Sugar (page 38) or granulated sugar*
> *1 cup warm milk*
> *½ cup melted butter*
> *1 teaspoon salt*
> *1 large egg*

Ground cinnamon, for sprinkling over the dough
1 egg yolk and 1 tablespoon milk, to brush over the cake
1 dried bean
Fondant Icing (page 39)

Sift 3 cups of the flour into a large mixing bowl and make a well in the center. Place the yeast and 1 tablespoon of the Vanilla Sugar in the well. Add the milk and stir to dissolve the yeast. Sprinkle a little flour over the yeast mixture, cover the bowl with a kitchen towel, and let it stand in a warm, draft-free place until the mixture becomes foamy, about 10 minutes.

In a small bowl, beat the butter, the remaining Vanilla Sugar, the salt and whole egg until blended. Stir the butter mixture into the flour-yeast mixture. Add the remaining flour ¼ cup at a time to make a soft dough.

Turn the dough out onto a lightly floured work surface. Knead the dough until it becomes smooth and elastic, about 5 minutes, incorporating more flour as needed. Shape the dough into a ball. Lightly grease a large bowl with butter and place the dough in the bowl. Turn the ball so that the surface is coated with butter. Cover the bowl with a towel and let the dough rise at room temperature until doubled in size, about 1½ hours.

Grease a large baking sheet. Divide the dough into 3 equal portions and sprinkle with cinnamon. Working with 1 portion at a time and using your hands, roll the dough into a 40-inch strand. Repeat with the remaining portions. Braid these 3 strands together, as you would long hair. Once the braid is formed, gently shape the dough into a large circle, pinching the ends together tightly to close the circle. (Alternately, leave the dough in 1 piece and shape into a large oval, approximately 14 inches in diameter.)

Place the King Cake on the greased baking sheet. Combine the egg yolk and milk in a small bowl to make an eggwash. Brush the cake with the egg wash, cover with a large kitchen towel, and allow to rise at room temperature for a second time, until doubled in bulk, about 1 hour.

Meanwhile, preheat the oven to 325°F. When ready, brush the cake with eggwash again and bake in the preheated oven for 45 minutes or until golden brown. While the cake is baking, make the Fondant Icing.

Remove the cake from the oven and gently push the dried bean into the bottom of the cake. Frost the cake with Fondant Icing while it is still warm. Cut the cake into slices and serve.

Makes 1 large cake

CON

DIMENTS
& sauces

IT SEEMS AS THOUGH every family in New Orleans has a fig tree in their back-yard, and each family has a favorite use for this delicious fruit—from jams to ice cream. I like making this fig conserve, which is delectable as a spread for morning toast and as a topping for ice creams and pound cake, as well as drying my own fresh figs. (I employ the methods outlined for the Oven-Dried Tomatoes on page 67, omitting the salt or sugar.) Home-dried figs are much healthier than most commercially available dried fruit, as the commercial products usually include nitrates.

If you don't like skin on your fruit, peel the figs before making this Fig Conserve.

2 pounds fresh figs, washed, stems removed, and quartered
1 cup brandy
4 cups granulated sugar
Juice of 1 lemon
½ teaspoon salt
1 cup chopped pecans

Sterilize three 1-cup jars and their lids according to the directions on page 134 and leave in the hot water.

Combine the figs, brandy, sugar, lemon juice, and salt in a medium-sized, heavy saucepan. Place the pan over medium-low heat and bring to a simmer, uncovered, until it reaches a threadlike consistency, about 30 minutes. From time to time skim any scum that may have formed on the surface and stir gently, being careful not to break the fruit.

Remove the pan from the heat and fold in the pecans. Pour the fig jam into the hot sterilized jars, leaving ⅛-inch headspace. Allow to sit for 2 weeks before using. Refrigerate after opening.

Makes 3 cups

pages 42–43: Cumberland Sauce

PONTCHATOULA, LOUISIANA (about 1 hour northeast of New Orleans), grows possibly the sweetest berries I've ever tasted. The town claims to be the "Strawberry Capital of the World," and its annual Strawberry Festival draws vast crowds eager to sample strawberries in every food and beverage imaginable. As much as I enjoy all the tasting at the festival, for me there is no better way to capture the goodness of this lush berry than in a simple jam, served with fresh, hot Pecan Biscuits (page 121).

4 pounds fresh, unbruised strawberries, washed and hulled
6 cups granulated sugar

Combine the berries and sugar in a large, heavy stockpot and allow to sit for 1 hour.

Sterilize four 1-pint jars and their lids according to the directions on page 134 and leave in the hot water.

Slowly bring the berries and sugar to boiling, stirring occasionally until the sugar dissolves, about 20 minutes. Cook the mixture over medium-high heat until thick, about 45 minutes, stirring from time to time. With a slotted spoon, remove any white residue that forms on the surface as the sugar cooks.

Remove the pot from the heat and pour the hot jam into the hot sterilized jars. Adjust the caps and seal. Store the jars in a cool, dry place. Refrigerate after opening.

Makes 4 pints

I FIND HONEY to have the purest flavor of all natural sweeteners and to be the best energy source imaginable. This flavored honey makes a delicious spread on morning toast or can be drizzled on hot oatmeal. If the honey crystallizes over time, place the whole jar in a bowl and surround with warm water. Allow the jar to sit in the water until the honey returns to its natural fluid state.

> *1 quart honey*
> *Zest of 1 orange, freshly grated*
> *Zest of 1 lemon, freshly grated*
> *Zest of 1 lime, freshly grated*
> *1 clove*
> *1 cinnamon stick, broken into pieces*
> *8 black peppercorns, crushed*
> *½ teaspoon fresh rosemary leaves*
> *¼ teaspoon dried lavender blossoms (page 34)*

Warm the honey in a large, heavy saucepan over low heat until it reaches 140°F. on a candy thermometer, about 2 minutes. Place the remaining ingredients in the center of a 10-inch square of cheesecloth and draw up the sides to form a pouch. Secure the cheesecloth sachet tightly with string and place in the pot with the honey. Continue warming the honey over low heat for 2 hours, stirring occasionally.

Sterilize two 1-pint jars and their lids according to the directions on page 134 and leave in the hot water.

Remove the pot with the honey from the heat and allow to cool slightly. Remove the sachet, squeeze to release any honey, and discard. Pour the honey into the hot, sterilized jars, leaving about ⅛-inch headspace. Store in a cool, dry place until ready to use.

Makes 2 pints

THIS IS A NICE ACCOMPANIMENT to meats, pâtés, and cheeses. I especially like to serve this jelly with roast lamb, adding 1 cup minced mint leaves during the final cooking process. For an easy snack, try a bit of Hot Pepper Jelly spread with Creole Cheese (page 20) on top of crackers or sliced bread.

If you want to make this jelly even spicier, add a pinch of red pepper flakes along with the sugar and vinegar.

>*7 cups finely chopped green bell peppers, cored and seeded (14 to 16 medium peppers)*
>*2 tablespoons salt*
>*6 cups granulated sugar*
>*4 cups apple cider vinegar*
>*12 jalapeño peppers, seeded and cored, finely diced*

Sterilize six 1-cup jars and their lids according to the directions on page 134 and leave in the hot water.

Place the bell peppers and salt in a large, heavy-bottomed pot and let stand 3 to 4 hours. Add the sugar and vinegar to the pot. Cook the mixture over low heat, stirring frequently, until thick, about 45 minutes. Skim the surface from time to time to remove any scum that may have formed.

Remove the pot from the heat and pour, boiling hot, into the sterilized jars, leaving ⅛-inch headspace. Adjust the lids and store in a cool, dry place until ready to use.

Makes 6 cups

NOW YOU CAN MAKE YOUR OWN hot pepper sauce, just like those famous Louisiana sauces. Blend to suit your tastes—whether fiery or mild—and mix into soups, sauces, and dressings. The chili pepper's heat comes from its seeds and surrounding white membranes. If you prefer a milder sauce, reduce the quantity of seeds called for here.

When chopping hot peppers always be very careful not to touch your eyes, nose, or mouth, and wash your hands and all utensils extremely well after handling.

Due to a shortage of large glass containers during and after the Civil War, Louisiana's most renowned hot sauce was originally packaged in cologne bottles, hence their shape today. If desired, continue the tradition and use decorative bottles for your homemade sauce.

After the bottle is opened, the hot sauce will naturally oxidize and begin to turn brown. This oxidization will also cause the sauce to get hotter.

4 cups finely chopped, ripe red chili peppers, stems removed, seeds remaining
8 cloves garlic, peeled
2 cups apple cider vinegar
1 tablespoon salt
1 tablespoon granulated sugar
1 clove
1 bay leaf
Pinch ground allspice

Sterilize six 1-cup jars or decorative bottles and their lids according to the directions on page 134 and leave in the hot water.

Place all of the ingredients in a large, heavy saucepan and slowly bring to a boil over medium-high heat. Reduce the heat to a simmer and cook, uncovered, for 5 minutes. Remove the pan from the heat and cool to room temperature. When cool, remove the bay leaf and clove with a slotted spoon and discard.

Place the hot sauce in a food processor (in 2 batches if necessary) and purée on high speed until smooth, about 2 minutes. Bottle the sauce in the hot jars and refrigerate until ready to use.

Makes 6 cups

RED BEANS ARE THE TRADITIONAL "Monday food" of southeastern Louisiana, immortalized in the well known dish Red Beans and Rice. The beans earned their nickname as they could be cooked slowly all day on the stovetop by wash women and housewives while the week's laundry was being done elsewhere in the house.

To give your beans more body and flavor, add diced leeks, carrots, or any other vegetable 15 minutes before the beans are done, and liberally splash each serving with Hot Pepper Sauce (page 50).

BEANS

1 cup dried red kidney beans

½ cup chopped bacon

1 cup sliced andouille or other hot smoked sausage

1 large yellow onion, peeled and finely chopped

½ cup diced celery

½ cup diced green bell pepper

1 teaspoon olive oil

3 cloves garlic, peeled and minced

1 medium bay leaf

1 sprig fresh thyme

1 teaspoon salt

½ teaspoon freshly ground black pepper

¼ teaspoon ground oregano

1 teaspoon Hot Pepper Sauce (page 50)

6 cups homemade Chicken Stock (page 132) or Vegetable Stock (page 133)
or canned reduced-sodium chicken broth

RICE

1 cup long-grain rice
Pinch salt
2 cups homemade Chicken Stock (page 132)
    or canned reduced-sodium chicken broth or water
1 medium bay leaf

Place the beans in a colander and pick over to remove any stones or discolored beans. Put the beans in a large stockpot, cover with fresh cold water, and soak for 3 hours or preferably overnight to expedite the cooking process.

Drain the beans. In a large stockpot, place the chopped bacon and sauté gently over medium heat to release the grease. Add the sausage and sauté for 4 minutes. Add the onion, celery, bell pepper, olive oil, garlic, bay leaf, thyme, salt, pepper, oregano, and hot pepper sauce. Sauté over medium heat for 2 minutes, stirring continuously. Add the beans and stock and bring to a simmer over medium heat. Cook, uncovered, until the beans are tender, about 45 minutes to 1 hour. Skim the surface occasionally to remove any scum.

About 20 minutes before the beans are ready, prepare the rice: Combine the rice, salt, stock, and bay leaf in a medium-sized, heavy-bottomed pot and cook slowly over low heat for about 15 to 17 minutes, or until the liquid is absorbed by the rice. Remove the pot from the heat, discard the bay leaf, and serve immediately with the red beans.

When the beans are tender, remove the pot from the heat and drain if necessary to get rid of any excess liquid. (The beans should have a creamy consistency.) Discard the bay leaf, season to taste, and serve immediately over rice.

Makes 4 to 6 servings

CONFIT, IN WHICH meat is cooked in its own fat, is probably one of the oldest forms for preserving food. The method of making confit presented here evolved in southwestern France and then made its way to southern Louisiana with the early French immigrants.

Domestic store-bought duck works well in this recipe because of its high fat content. The ideal ratio when making confit is 55 percent meat to 45 percent fat. The thigh is the most desirable part of the duck as it has the most flavor. Be sure you leave the meat on the bone before packing in jars; otherwise, the meat will need to be recooked later.

While traditional confit recipes, which were written prior to refrigeration and always made during the cold wintertime months, call for allowing the confit to sit at room temperature for several months before use, I suggest you refrigerate the confit while it rests.

Duck confit is an ideal picnic food, served with fresh, crusty French bread and Creole Mustard (page 57), or serve it hot with boiled new potatoes and freshly ground black pepper. You can also use the preserved confit to make cassoulet, the hearty French dish featuring white beans and meat.

2 4-pound ducks, cleaned
5 cups kosher or sea salt
1 teaspoon ground allspice
6 crushed bay leaves

Rinse the ducks under cold running water and pat dry. Combine the salt, allspice, and bay leaves in a large bowl or roasting pan. Cut the whole ducks into quarters and place in the bowl with the spices, tossing to coat well. Cover the ducks with a kitchen towel and allow to sit at room temperature for 28 hours.

Preheat the oven to its lowest setting.

Rinse the ducks thoroughly under cold running water to remove the seasonings and pat dry. Layer the duck pieces in a deep, heavy roasting pan and place in the oven. Roast the duck until the meat is tender and falls off the bone, about 12 hours. Remove the pan from the oven and let sit until the meat is cool enough to handle.

Sterilize three 1-pint jars and their lids according to the directions on page 134 and leave in the hot water.

Remove the cooled duck pieces from the pot and place in the hot, sterilized jars. Cover the duck completely with the rendered fat remaining in the roasting pan, and seal the jars. Allow the confit to rest in the refrigerator for 3 to 4 months before eating.

Makes 3 pints

THERE ARE MANY USES for ground mustard seeds. To make Creole Mustard, see page 57. To make your own yellow table mustard, simply stir either milk or yogurt, 1 teaspoon at a time, into a small bowl of the ground seeds and blend until a paste is achieved. This homemade mustard is excellent with steaks. Alternatively, instead of grinding the toasted mustard seeds, sprinkle them on salads for a tasty crunch. Or try an old remedy for relieving colds and clearing stuffy sinuses. Add 1 tablespoon of ground mustard to a pot of boiling water. Remove the pot from the stove, put a towel over your head and the pot, and breathe in the steam.

1 cup yellow mustard seeds

Heat a heavy skillet over medium heat and add the mustard seeds. Cook, uncovered, until the seeds begin to pop, about 1 minute. Remove the skillet from the heat and cover with a kitchen towel until the popping stops and the seeds cool, about 5 minutes.

Place the toasted mustard seeds in an airtight container to be used later, or grind them with a mortar and pestle for use in other recipes. (If you don't have or want to use a mortar and pestle, place the seeds between 2 sheets of waxed paper and grind with a rolling pin on a flat surface.)

Makes 1 cup

THIS IS SIMILAR to the whole-grain mustards from the town of Dijon, France. It was probably brought to Louisiana by the French-descended Acadians (Cajuns) who migrated to this area from Canada 200 years ago. Today in South Louisiana it's a popular addition to our French bread "Po' Boy" sandwiches—whether oyster, shrimp, or roast beef—and a full-flavored component in sauces. You might try adding a teaspoon to your salad dressings for extra bite and a little texture.

> *1 cup dry white wine*
> *1 clove garlic, peeled and minced*
> *1 teaspoon celery seeds*
> *1 teaspoon ground allspice*
> *½ teaspoon salt*
> *¼ teaspoon ground cloves*
> *Pinch nutmeg or mace*
> *1 cup Ground Mustard Seeds (page 55)*
> *2 tablespoons tarragon vinegar*
> *2 tablespoons malt vinegar*

Sterilize three 1-cup jars and their lids according to the instructions on page 134 and leave in the hot water.

Combine the white wine, garlic, celery seeds, allspice, salt, cloves, and nutmeg in a small, heavy saucepan. Bring the mixture to a simmer over medium-high heat. Remove the pan from the heat and allow to sit, uncovered, for 2 hours.

In a large bowl, mix the ground mustard seeds and tarragon and malt vinegars until you have a smooth paste. Return the pot with the wine infusion to a boil over high heat. Remove the pan from the heat and strain through a fine sieve into the bowl with the mustard paste. Mix well, stirring constantly. Pour the mustard into the hot, sterilized jars, leaving ⅛-inch headspace, and adjust the lids. Store in a cool, dry place for 3 weeks before use. Refrigerate after opening.

Makes 3 cups

THIS RÉMOULADE SAUCE IS most often served as an accompaniment to seafood; it is not usually mixed in with other ingredients, as is the fashion with Creole Rémoulade (opposite).

1 cup homemade Mayonnaise (page 124) or store-bought mayonnaise
1 teaspoon chopped capers
1 teaspoon chopped cornichons (pickled gherkins)
1 teaspoon minced parsley
1 teaspoon chopped, drained anchovy fillet or anchovy paste

Place all of the ingredients in a mixing bowl and stir to mix. Serve with seafood.

Makes 1 cup

AGAIN, A CREOLE VARIATION on a French staple; this time a sauce for seafood and cold meats. The Creole incarnation is most often tossed with boiled shrimp or crawfish tails and served on a bed of lettuce as an appetizer or light lunch.

As with homemade Mayonnaise (page 124), this sauce will separate after refrigeration; this is not a sign that it is going bad. Simply beat the sauce back together before mixing with seafood or serving with other dishes.

> *2 cloves garlic, peeled and minced*
> *1 hard-boiled egg, finely chopped*
> *3 anchovy fillets, drained and minced*
> *¾ cup pure olive oil*
> *¼ cup Creole Tomato Ketchup (page 61) or store-bought ketchup*
> *¼ cup minced parsley*
> *3 tablespoons Creole Mustard (page 57) or Dijon mustard*
> *2 tablespoons malt vinegar*
> *1 tablespoon Ground Mustard Seeds (page 55)*
> *1 tablespoon fresh lemon juice*
> *1 tablespoon paprika*
> *2 dashes Worcestershire Sauce*
> *Salt to taste*
> *Freshly ground black pepper to taste*

Place all of the ingredients in the bowl of a food processor or blender. Purée on high speed until well blended, about 20 seconds. Serve with boiled or deep-fried shellfish. Store in an airtight container in the refrigerator for up to 2 weeks.

Makes 2 cups

THIS SAUCE IS EXCELLENT SERVED with fowl and game, which are abundant in Louisiana, a state sometimes referred to as "Sportsman's Paradise," for its diversity of wildlife and prime hunting and fishing. You might also want to try this sauce with cold smoked meat, ham, or pâté.

> ¼ *cup finely chopped shallots*
> *Zest of 1 orange*
> *1 16-ounce jar red currant jelly*
> *1 cup port wine*
> *Juice of 1 orange*
> *Juice of ½ lemon*
> *1 teaspoon Ground Mustard Seeds (page 55)*

Place 2 cups water in a medium-sized saucepan and bring to a boil over high heat. Add the chopped shallots to the water, return to a boil, and cook for 30 seconds. Quickly remove the shallots from the water with a slotted spoon and shock in ice water. Drain and dry the shallots on kitchen towels and set aside. Repeat the process with the orange zest and set aside.

Place the red currant jelly in a large, heavy saucepan and gently melt over low heat, stirring occasionally, about 5 minutes. Remove from the heat and set aside.

Sterilize three 1-cup jars and their lids according to the directions on page 134 and leave in the hot water.

Add the wine, orange and lemon juices, ground mustard, shallots, and zest to the red currant jelly. Mix well. Return the pan to the stove and gently warm through over low heat. Remove the pan from the heat and allow to cool to room temperature. Pour the Cumberland Sauce into the hot jars, leaving ⅛-inch headspace. Adjust the caps and refrigerate until ready to use, up to 2 months.

Makes 3 cups

KETCHUP IS ONE OF THE FEW bottled sauces that has attained worldwide acceptance and appears to satisfy a universal taste. While I enjoy commercial brands of ketchup, the piquancy of the fresh condiment just can't be duplicated in a ready-made product with a long shelf-life. You can use this Creole Tomato Ketchup on everything. It makes a great dipping sauce for boiled seafood or can be jazzed up into Creole Cocktail Sauce (page 64) or French Cocktail Sauce (page 63). Also try stirring minced, seeded fresh jalapeños into your ketchup. Or add minced basil, mint, thyme, or any other fresh herb to the ketchup during the final 5 minutes of cooking.

To set the ketchup's color, dissolve 1 crushed Vitamin C tablet in the warm ketchup. Store in the refrigerator for up to 1 month.

> **4 pounds Creole tomatoes or other variety of vine-ripened tomatoes,**
>   **cored and chopped**
> **2 cups granulated sugar**
> **¾ cup malt or apple cider vinegar**
> **½ teaspoon salt**
> **About 1 tablespoon Hot Pepper Sauce (page 50), optional**

Combine the chopped tomatoes, sugar, and vinegar in a large bowl and mash to a pulp with your hands or a potato masher. Place the tomato mixture and all of the remaining ingredients in a large, heavy, nonreactive saucepan. Cook the mixture slowly over low heat until the purée is thick and bubbly, about 1½ hours. Remove the pan from the heat and pass through a sieve into a clean bowl.

Allow the ketchup to cool, then serve or store in an airtight container in the refrigerator until ready to use.

Makes 3 cups

POTTED *crawfish*

POTTING, OR COVERING FOOD WITH BUTTER to seal it from the air, is an old European technique for preserving food. In this simplification of the technique—actually a takeoff on the English Potted Shrimp—crawfish is coated in a seasoned butter mixture. This dish is deceptively rich and makes a heavenly first course when served with hot toast points. Try making Potted Crawfish with your own butter, using the recipe on page 120.

While the yellow tomalley found in the head of the crawfish is most commonly called fat, it actually is the liver and pancreas of the shellfish. When using freshly boiled crawfish, extract this yellow substance and add it to the potting mixture for extra flavor.

If you are using frozen crawfish tail meat, refresh it in boiling water for 15 seconds, then plunge into ice water. Drain well and pat dry prior to adding it to the other ingredients.

Potted Crawfish will keep for up to 1 week in the refrigerator, but this dish is far better when eaten right away.

> *1 stick (½ cup) unsalted butter*
> *2 tablespoons Creole Tomato Ketchup (page 61) or store-bought ketchup*
> *2 tablespoons crawfish fat (if available)*
> *2 tablespoons fresh lemon juice*
> *Dash Hot Pepper Sauce (page 50)*
> *Pinch grated nutmeg*
> *Salt to taste*
> *12 ounces cooked crawfish tails*
> *Toast points, for serving*

Bring all of the ingredients to room temperature.

Cream the butter by hand until it reaches the consistency of mayonnaise. Add the Creole Ketchup, crawfish fat (if using), lemon juice, Hot Pepper Sauce, and nutmeg, and blend to form a smooth paste. Season with salt to taste.

Blend the crawfish meat into the butter mixture. Pack into four ½-cup ramekins. Chill for about 20 minutes or until firm. Serve at room temperature in the molds with toast points, or unmold, spread on toast and run under the broiler for 2 minutes.

Makes 4 servings / 2 cups

THIS CREAMY COCKTAIL SAUCE, with its mayonnaise base, is more refined and less spicy than the Creole Cocktail Sauce that follows. Both are delicious with fresh seafood.

1 cup homemade Mayonnaise (page 124) or store-bought mayonnaise
½ cup Creole Tomato Ketchup (page 61) or store-bought ketchup
¼ cup heavy cream
¼ cup minced yellow onion
¼ cup minced fresh pineapple and/or mango
1 tablespoon brandy
Dash Worcestershire sauce
Dash Hot Pepper Sauce (page 50)

Place all of the ingredients in the bowl of a food processor or blender and blend on high speed for 30 seconds.

Serve as an accompaniment to fresh seafood.

Makes 2 cups

FRENCH cocktail sauce

CREOLE *cocktail sauce*

THE RITUALS PEOPLE IN LOUISIANA go through to get their cocktail sauce just right never cease to amaze me. It seems everyone likes to blend cocktail sauce precisely to his or her own taste, adding a bit more hot sauce and a touch less horseradish or ketchup than the next person. Or they may add freshly squeezed lemon juice. Whatever your taste, blend your cocktail sauce to your liking and serve it with fresh seafood, especially raw or fried oysters or boiled shrimp.

3 cups Creole Tomato Ketchup (page 61) or store-bought ketchup
¼ cup prepared horseradish sauce
Dash Worcestershire sauce
Dash Hot Pepper Sauce (page 50)

Combine all of the ingredients in a mixing bowl, stirring well to mix. Serve with seafood or refrigerate in an airtight container until ready to use. This sauce will keep for 1 month in the refrigerator.

Makes 3 cups

AFTER MAKING YOUR OWN BARBEQUE SAUCE, you'll discover what you've been missing in those commercial brands—flavor! If you like spicy foods, add a bit of Hot Pepper Sauce (page 50).

Many people marinate their meat and poultry in barbeque sauce prior to grilling, but this type of "cold" marination doesn't work well since the texture of cold meat is resilient to flavor infusion unless the meat's acidic balance is altered (for instance, by citric juices or vinegars). To counteract this problem, I warm the barbeque sauce prior to brushing it on room-temperature meat.

¼ cup vegetable shortening or bacon grease
2 small yellow onions, peeled and minced
8 cloves garlic, peeled and minced
2 cups tomato purée
½ cup Steen's pure cane syrup or blackstrap molasses
½ cup apple cider vinegar
¼ cup Ground Mustard Seeds (page 55)
2 bay leaves
2 tablespoons dark brown sugar
2 tablespoons Worcestershire sauce
½ teaspoon ground cumin
½ teaspoon ground coriander
½ teaspoon freshly ground black pepper
½ teaspoon salt
¼ teaspoon cayenne pepper

Heat oil in a large, heavy saucepan over medium-high heat. Add the onions and garlic to the pan and sauté until tender, about 2 minutes. Add the tomato purée and cook until the purée begins to turn brown, about 5 minutes, stirring constantly.

Add the remaining ingredients and bring to a boil over high heat. Reduce the heat to a simmer and cook gently for 1 hour, stirring from time to time.

Meanwhile, sterilize three 1-pint jars and their lids according to the directions on page 134 and leave in the hot water.

When ready, remove the sauce from the heat and allow to cool slightly before using. Or bottle in the sterilized jars and adjust the caps. Refrigerate for later use.

Makes 3 pint

AS TOMATOES DRY IN THE OVEN, they shrivel and toughen slightly, their red color deepens, and their flavor intensifies. Dried tomatoes can be used to add a concentrated tomato taste to pasta dishes, pizza, focaccia, and salads, and, believe it or not, are terrific shredded and sprinkled on vanilla ice cream!

Instead of storing oven-dried tomatoes in olive oil or in an airtight container at room temperature, try keeping them in the freezer, where they will hold their flavor and their rich ruby color longer.

This recipe can also be used to dry many varieties of fruit, such as grapes, apples, and pineapple. Simply follow the method outlined here, omitting the salt.

> *2 pounds firm plum tomatoes, washed and dried, stems removed*
> *1 teaspoon salt*
> *1 teaspoon granulated sugar*

Preheat the oven to its lowest setting.

Cut the tomatoes in half lengthwise and place on a wire rack on a baking sheet, skin-side down. Combine the salt and sugar and sprinkle lightly over the tomatoes. Place the tomatoes in the oven and bake until shriveled and slightly tough, about 12 to 14 hours. Remove the tomatoes from the oven and cool on wire racks. Store in airtight containers in the freezer until ready to use.

Makes 12 ounces

BEV

ERAGES
& snacks

NOTHING IS QUITE AS REFRESHING on a hot day as a tart, homemade lemonade served over ice. And there are countless variations to this lemonade theme. For instance, split a vanilla pod down the center and scrape out the tiny seeds. Add the vanilla seeds and the split pod to the water. Allow to cool, remove the pod, then add the sugar and lemon juice. Chill for a bracing Vanilla Lemonade. Or try adding herbs to your infusion. One cup of shredded basil added to 2 quarts of water will give you Basil Lemonade.

Cold lemonade is also a great source of Vitamin C. Since it isn't heated, none of the natural vitamins present in the lemon juice are destroyed.

2 cups granulated sugar
13 lemons, washed and dried

Spread the sugar evenly on a clean, flat working surface. Roll 1 lemon into the sugar, pressing hard with the palm of your hand so as to release the oils from the lemon. Set aside and repeat with 11 lemons.

Place a fine strainer over a medium mixing bowl. Halve each lemon crosswise and squeeze the juice into the bowl, so the strainer will catch the seeds and any pulp. Discard the lemon pulp, seeds, and rind.

Combine the lemon juice, sugar, and 2 quarts cold water in a large pitcher and stir well to dissolve the sugar. Chill the lemonade in the refrigerator for 2 hours.

With a sharp knife, cut long, decorative twists from the remaining lemon by cutting thin strips of skin from around the circumference of the fruit. Pour the lemonade into glasses over crushed ice, and garnish the rim of each glass with a decorative twist. Serve.

Makes 2 quarts

preceding pages: Cold Lemonade and Cat's Tongue Cookies

I REMEMBER DRINKING PRODIGIOUS QUANTITIES of this hot drink whenever I had a cold as a child. I'm not sure if there are actually any medicinal benefits but, like many home remedies, this one always seemed to make me feel better. When serving to adults, add a shot of brandy as you strain the lemonade into the glass.

> *12 lemons, quartered*
> *2 cups honey*
> *1 clove*

Combine all of the ingredients with 2 quarts water in a large, heavy saucepan. Bring the mixture to a boil over high heat and cook, uncovered, for 10 minutes. Remove the pan from the heat and allow to cool until it reaches a drinkable temperature.

Strain into mugs and serve hot. Refrigerate any leftover lemonade to be reheated later on or to be served as cold lemonade.

Makes 2 quarts

THIS BEER IS WONDERFUL over crushed ice on hot days. I like mine spicy, but you can reduce the amount of ginger to suit your taste. This is a popular drink not only in Louisiana but in the West Indies and Europe as well.

It is important that you use spring or purified water in this recipe as it gives the beer a smoother flavor than tap water. Note that this beer does indeed "pack a punch," with about four degrees of alcohol, and should be served to adults only.

With the newfound popularity of home-brewing it is easy to obtain beer bottles and the appropriate tops from mail-order catalogs or in hardware stores. Make sure the tops are well affixed to the bottles; otherwise, as the beer ferments, it will bubble out of the bottles.

> *2 tablespoons fresh, peeled and minced gingerroot*
> *8 cups spring water*
> *Zest of 2 lemons*
> *Juice of 1 lemon*
> *1½ cups granulated sugar*
> *2 tablespoons cream of tartar*
> *½ teaspoon active dry yeast*

Place the ginger in a large stockpot and set aside. Pour 8 cups spring water into a clean pot and quickly bring to a boil over high heat. Pour the water over the ginger and stir. Add the lemon zest, lemon juice, sugar, and cream of tartar to the ginger pot and stir until the sugar has completely dissolved.

Combine 1 teaspoon of the ginger syrup with the yeast in a small bowl and stir until the yeast has dissolved, about 2 minutes. Add the yeast to the large pot with the ginger mixture. Cover the pot with plastic wrap and allow to sit for 4 hours.

Sterilize four 1-pint bottles and their tops according to the directions on page 134 and leave in the hot water.

Pour the ginger beer into the sterilized bottles, filling nearly to the top. Firmly attach a metal cap to each bottle and allow to ferment in a cool, dark place for 6 weeks. Chill well before serving.

Makes 4 pints

SERVE THESE FLAVORFUL PUMPKIN SEEDS with cocktails or sprinkle in green salads for a delicious crunch.

> *3 cups raw pumpkin seeds*
> *½ egg white*
> *¼ cup granulated sugar*
> *1 tablespoon salt*
> *1 teaspoon paprika*
> *¼ teaspoon cayenne pepper*

Preheat the oven to 375°F. Line a baking sheet with parchment paper and set aside.

Combine the pumpkin seeds and egg white in a large, stainless-steel bowl and toss to coat. Sprinkle the sugar, salt, paprika, and cayenne pepper over the seeds and toss well to coat evenly. Spread the seeds on the baking sheet and bake for 5 minutes in the preheated oven. Remove the baking sheet from the oven and shake to keep the seeds from sticking together. Repeat this process twice more, baking for 5 minutes each time and shaking. Remove from the oven and allow to cool on the baking sheet. Serve warm or store indefinitely in an airtight container at room temperature.

Makes 3 cups

MINT Julep

WHILE THE MINT JULEP is inextricably linked to Kentucky and Derby Day, it is a popular drink throughout the South, Louisiana included. There's something very invigorating about a Mint Julep on a hot afternoon, with its crushed ice and refreshing mint. This drink is traditionally served in a sterling Mint Julep cup, but a double old-fashioned glass will do. For added spiciness, try making your Mint Julep with fresh peppermint leaves instead of spearmint.

4 sprigs fresh spearmint or peppermint, washed
1 teaspoon granulated sugar
1 jigger (2½ ounces) bourbon whiskey

Remove the leaves from 3 mint sprigs and mince. Combine the minced mint leaves and sugar in a glass and mix to a paste with the back of a spoon. Add crushed ice to fill the glass halfway, then pour the bourbon over the ice. Stir well. Decorate the glass with the remaining mint sprig and serve.

Makes 1 drink

SERVE THIS LIQUEUR after dinner and recall the glory days of New Orleans, with its genteel home entertaining and lavish carnival and opera balls. Note that the longer you keep Orange Blossom Liqueur, the better it will taste, as the flavors will continue to marry even after the bottle has been opened. Fresh orange blossoms are available at specialty food stores.

> *10 ounces fresh orange blossoms*
> *1 teaspoon ground cinnamon*
> *1 clove*
> *3½ cups light rum*
> *2½ cups packed dark brown sugar*

Combine the orange blossoms, cinnamon, clove, and rum in a large glass jar and seal. Place the jar in a cool, dark place and allow to sit for 1 month.

Sterilize one 1-quart bottle and its lid according to the directions on page 134 and leave in the hot water.

Combine the brown sugar and 2 cups water in a small, heavy saucepan. Bring the mixture to a boil over high heat, then remove from the heat and allow to cool. Combine the sugar water with the orange blossom mixture, then strain through a paper coffee filter into the sterilized bottle. Adjust the lid.

Store in a cool, dark place for 6 months before serving. Serve after dinner with dessert and coffee.

Makes 1 quart

BELIEVE IT OR NOT, voodoo practitioners still exist in New Orleans. Like their eighteenth- and nineteenth-century predecessors, they are called upon to perform myriad services—from dispelling evil spirits and setting spells on hated rivals to concocting love potions. This elixir is of my own devising, and while I can't guarantee its infallibility in enticing love your way, I can assure you that it is a novel and tasty aperitif. Try serving it to your intended and see what happens.

> *2 tablespoons Spiced Honey (page 48) or plain honey*
> *1 teaspoon Kumquat-Flavored Rum (page 79) or light rum*
> *10 shredded rose petals*
> *2 mint leaves*
> *Pinch cayenne pepper*
> *6 ounces Champagne*
> *2 fresh raspberries*

Place the honey, rum, rose petals, mint leaves, and cayenne pepper in a small saucepan. Warm the mixture over low heat until the honey begins to run. Remove the pan from the heat and stir. Allow the honey to cool slightly.

   Strain the honey mixture into a tall, fluted glass and add the Champagne. Stir twice, then add the raspberries to the glass. Serve immediately.

Makes 1 drink

WITH THE ABUNDANCE OF SUGAR CANE throughout Louisiana, cane liquor was in great supply in days past. I'm sure the Creoles came up with many flavors to infuse into their liquor, and what fun they must have had experimenting. This flavored rum makes an unbelievably good piña colada cocktail or can be served on its own over finely crushed ice. You might also try it as a liqueur after dinner or even cook with it, instead of the usual sherry or brandy. As with regular distilled spirits, Kumquat-Flavored Rum will keep indefinitely when stored properly in an airtight bottle. If kumquats aren't to your liking or are not available in your area, try using fresh raspberries.

> *1 12-inch square cheesecloth*
> *1 pound fresh kumquats, washed and diced*
> *1 quart light rum*

Place the cheesecloth square flat on a work surface. Into the center of the cloth place the cut kumquats. Gather up the cloth to form a bundle, twisting up the ends. Tie the bundle tightly with a string, leaving about 12 inches of string so you can suspend the bundle from the top of the jar.

Pour the rum into a large glass jar. Suspend the kumquat bundle 1-inch over the rum and tie the extra string securely around the top of the jar. Seal the top of the jar with plastic wrap and secure tightly with a rubber band to make the jar airtight. Place the jar in a cool, dark place for 2 weeks. (The jar must be tightly sealed in order for the fruit essences to permeate the liquor.)

After 2 weeks remove the plastic wrap and kumquat bundle from the jar and discard, being careful not to let the fruit touch the surface of the rum at any time during this process. Transfer the rum to an airtight bottle.

Makes 1 quart

MINCEMEAT

THOUGH PRETTY RARE THESE DAYS, mincemeat pie is one of my favorite desserts during the Christmas season. I think this dish has lost its popularity because of the low quality and inferior taste of the mincemeat sold commercially.

Originally mince pies were made with ox tongue, chicken, eggs, lemon peel, onions, and spices. Over time the eggs, onion, and meat were eliminated, save the suet, which is essential to the flavor.

Suet is animal fat, and the best is taken from around the kidney, as it is the whitest and most pure. Obtain it from your local butcher and ask him or her to grind it finely for you.

If you're feeling especially festive, give the mixture an extra splash of brandy before packing into the jars. Note that the longer the mincemeat sits before being cooked into pies, the better it will be. When I was growing up, we always made ours in January for use the following December.

> *2 cups peeled and finely chopped Granny Smith apples*
> *1½ cups shredded or ground suet*
> *1½ cups seedless golden raisins*
> *1½ cups Sultana raisins*
> *1 cup granulated sugar*
> *⅓ cup mixed candied fruit peel*
> *2 tablespoons brandy*
> *2 tablespoons Kumquat-Flavored Rum (page 79) or light rum*
> *Juice and zest of 1 lemon*
> *½ teaspoon ground cinnamon*
> *½ teaspoon ground cloves*
> *½ teaspoon ground nutmeg*
> *½ teaspoon ground mace*

Sterilize four 1-pint jars and their lids according to the directions on page 134 and leave in the hot water.

Combine all of the ingredients in a large bowl and mix well. Pack the mincemeat into the hot jars and adjust the lids. Allow to cool and store in the refrigerator until ready to bake into pies, up to 1 year.

Makes 8 cups

Using Mincemeat

> 2¼ cups all-purpose flour
> ½ cup Homemade Sweet Butter (page 120)
>   or unsalted butter, at room temperature
> 2 large eggs, beaten
> 3 tablespoons Vanilla Sugar (page 38) or granulated sugar
> ¼ teaspoon salt
> 2 to 3 tablespoons cold water
> 1½ cups homemade Mincemeat (opposite)
>   or store-bought mincemeat
> 1-2 tablespoons milk

Sift the flour into a large mixing bowl and make a well in the center. Add the butter, eggs, sugar, and salt to the center of the well and mix together with your hands to form a dough. If the pastry is too crumbly, add cold water, 1 teaspoon at a time, to reach the correct consistency, being careful not to overwork the dough.

Form the dough into a ball, wrap in plastic, and refrigerate for 1 hour.

Preheat the oven to 375°F.

Divide the dough into 2 equal parts. On a lightly floured surface, roll out 1 ball of dough into a ¼-inch-thick circle. Line the bottom of a 9-inch pie pan with the dough, leaving a ¼-inch overhang.

Place the mincemeat on the dough in the pan. Roll out the remaining ball of dough to a thickness of ¼ inch and cover the mincemeat filling with this dough. Fold the overhanging edge of the first dough over that of the second to seal. Crimp the edge of the pie with a fork to completely seal the filling. Cut slits into the top crust of the pie and brush the crust with the milk.

Place the pie in the preheated oven and bake for 30 to 40 minutes or until the top crust is golden brown. Remove the pie from the oven and allow to cool 30 minutes before cutting. Serve either warm or at room temperature.

Makes 1 (9-inch) pie

EGGNOG IS SERVED IN SOUTH LOUISIANA at the traditional multi-course Christmas Eve dinner known as *reveillon*. For added flavor, scrape the seeds from a split vanilla pod as well as the pod itself into the saucepan when cooking the milk. Remove the pod prior to mixing the milk with the egg yolk mixture. Try dipping Cat's Tongue Cookies (opposite) into your Eggnog for an especially delicious treat.

> *6 eggs, separated*
> *1 cup granulated sugar*
> *2 cups whole milk*
> *¼ cup brandy, rum, or bourbon whiskey*
> *Dash grated nutmeg*

Combine the egg yolks and sugar in a mixing bowl and beat until the yolks turn white. In a separate bowl, whip the egg whites to a stiff peak and set aside.

Place the milk in a heavy saucepan and bring to a boil over high heat. Quickly remove the pan from the heat. Slowly pour the hot milk into the bowl with the egg yolks, whipping constantly. When the milk has been incorporated, gently fold the egg whites into the yolk mixture, then add the brandy.

Serve the Eggnog warm or chill and serve later. Sprinkle with nutmeg before serving.

Makes 5 cups

THESE BUTTERY COOKIES are a wonderful accompaniment to coffee, tea, dessert wines, and Champagne, as well as to Eggnog.

> 2 sticks (1 cup) Homemade Sweet Butter (page 120)
>   or unsalted butter, at room temperature
> 2½ cups sifted powdered sugar
> 5 egg whites
> 3 cups sifted all-purpose flour
> ¼ teaspoon vanilla extract

Line a large baking sheet with greased parchment paper and set aside.

Preheat the oven to 400°F.

Using an electric mixer, cream the butter with the sugar. At low speed and one at a time, add the egg whites to the bowl and mix just to partially blend. Gently fold the flour and vanilla extract into the mixture, being careful not to overmix.

Place the cookie dough in a pastry bag fitted with a ⅛-inch diameter tip. Pipe even 2-inch lengths of cookie dough, 1 inch apart, onto the greased parchment paper. Place the baking sheet in the oven and bake the cookies until the edges just begin to brown, about 5 to 10 minutes. Remove the cookies from the oven and allow to cool on wire racks.

Serve the warm cookies with Eggnog. Store in an airtight container at room temperature for up to 4 days or in the refrigerator for longer.

Makes approximately 3 dozen

THESE TRADITIONAL CANDIES make festive holiday snacks for the little ones—and their adult friends! Or serve these with coffee after dinner.

Popcorn balls will keep for 1 week in an airtight container at room temperature.

> *½ cup granulated sugar*
> *2 tablespoons Kumquat-Flavored Rum (page 79) or light rum*
> *1 teaspoon Homemade Sweet Butter (page 120) or unsalted butter*
> *8 cups popped corn*
> *Powdered sugar, for dusting*

Combine the sugar and rum with 2 tablespoons water in a large, heavy saucepan. Cook over medium heat until the water evaporates and the sugar begins to caramelize and turn a golden brown, about 10 minutes.

Remove the pan from the heat and add the butter, stirring constantly to form a caramel. Fold the popped corn into the caramel, stirring so the caramel coats the popcorn. When cool enough to handle, scoop the caramel corn with a tablespoon and roll out on waxed paper into balls.

Lightly dust the candied popcorn balls with powdered sugar and serve.

Makes 16 popcorn balls

RUM-DRIED grapes (raisins)

GRAPE-GROWING IS RATHER COMMON in Southeast Louisiana. In fact, a neighbor of mine grows a bountiful crop every year, although the wild birds generally end up with a good portion of them. My neighbor makes grape jelly with his share. With the portion he gives me, I make raisins.

Not all grapes are suitable for raisins, but a rule of thumb is to choose a sweet variety that is relatively thin-skinned. Enjoy these raisins as a snack, mix them into vanilla ice cream or cookie or cake batter, or dip them in chocolate for a rich dessert treat.

5 pounds red seedless grapes, washed and stemmed
1 cup Kumquat-Flavored Rum (page 79) or light rum

Preheat the oven to "warm" or its lowest setting.

Line a large baking sheet with parchment paper. Place the grapes on the parchment paper and put in the oven to dry for 12 hours or overnight.

Place the rum in a mixing bowl. Remove the dried grapes (raisins) from the oven and place in the bowl with the rum, stirring to coat evenly. Allow the raisins to sit for 1 hour. Drain the raisins in a sieve and discard the rum. Place the raisins on the parchment-covered baking sheet and return to the oven to dry for 24 to 36 hours.

Remove the raisins from the oven and place in an airtight container. The raisins will keep indefinitely in an airtight container at room temperature.

Makes 2 cups

86 · BEVERAGES & SNACKS

THIS TOMATO JUICE makes a refreshing drink plain or served with vodka as a cocktail. You might also want to try it chilled as a light summer soup. Use tomatoes that are almost overripe, as they will yield the most juice. The residual tomatoes are discarded after making the juice, as no flavor will be left, only a bland pulp.

> *5 pounds very ripe tomatoes*
> *1 tablespoon salt*
> *1 tablespoon chopped fresh basil or tarragon leaves*

Line a large stainless-steel bowl or pot with a 3-foot square piece of cheesecloth. Place the tomatoes in the center of the cloth and gently crush them with your hands. Sprinkle the salt and chopped herbs into the tomatoes and mix with your hands. Bring up the corners of the cloth to form a bundle and tightly secure with string. Suspend the tomato bundle from a hook and allow to drip naturally into a large bowl in a cool, dark place for 24 hours.

Pour the juice into glass containers and refrigerate for up to 7 days. Discard the tomatoes. Serve the juice chilled.

Makes 6 cups

OILS

VINEGARS
& dressings

I LIKE THIS VINEGAR because it imparts a distinctive, mild garlic flavor to salad dressings. You can easily vary the flavor by steeping ½ cup of any herb, such as rosemary or thyme, in it. Place the herb in a cheesecloth bag, drop the herb in the boiling vinegar, and steep for 5 minutes. (If you leave the herb in the vinegar for longer than 5 minutes the result will be bitter.)

> *8 cups apple cider or malt vinegar*
> *1 cup peeled and separated garlic cloves*
> *¼ cup granulated sugar*

Sterilize four 1-pint bottles and their lids according to the directions on page 134 and leave in the hot water.

Combine the vinegar, garlic, and sugar in a large nonreactive pot. Bring to rolling boil over high heat and cook for 10 minutes. Remove the pot from the heat and allow to cool.

Strain the cooled vinegar through a sieve. Carefully divide the garlic cloves among the sterilized bottles. Pour the cooled vinegar over the garlic and fill each bottle, leaving ⅛-inch headspace. Seal the bottles, adjust the lids, and sterilize in a hot water bath for 10 minutes according to the directions on page 135. Store in a cool, dry place.

Makes 4 cups

THIS VINEGAR IS GREAT drizzled over grilled chicken with fresh raspberries served on the side. Also try a splash on a spinach salad or mix 1 teaspoon into other dressings or even into iced tea.

2 pints fresh, well-rinsed raspberries
4 cups red wine vinegar

Place the raspberries in a large, stainless-steel bowl and cover with the vinegar. Cover the bowl with plastic wrap and allow to macerate for 10 days. (Be careful not to stir while the vinegar is resting; this will bruise the berries.)

Sterilize four 1-cup jars or decorative bottles and their lids according to the directions on page 134 and leave in the hot water.

Strain the vinegar through a fine sieve, being careful not to break the fruit. Divide the raspberries among the sterilized bottles. Pour the vinegar over the berries and fill each bottle, leaving ⅛-inch headspace. Seal the bottles, adjust the lids, and sterilize in a hot water bath for 10 minutes according to the instructions on page 135. Store in a cool, dry place and allow to sit for 6 weeks before using.

Makes 2 pints

overleaf: Raspberry Vinegar

HONEY AND TARRAGON give this vinegar a smooth (not overly acidic) flavor. Try using it on summer salads, such as tomatoes with mozzarella cheese. Leave the seeds in the chopped jalapeño when cooking the vinegar, as this is what adds the desired heat.

> *8 cups malt vinegar*
> *2 cups honey*
> *1 cup chopped fresh jalapeño peppers, stems removed*
> *4 large tomatoes, seeded, cored, and roughly chopped*
> *4 large sprigs fresh tarragon with leaves attached, rinsed*

Sterilize four 1-pint bottles and their lids according to the instructions on page 134 and leave in the hot water.

Combine the vinegar, honey, and chopped peppers in a large nonreactive pot. Bring to a simmer over medium-high heat. Add the tomatoes and simmer until the tomatoes are soft, about 7 to 10 minutes. Remove the pot from the heat. Remove the tomatoes with a slotted spoon and discard. Allow the vinegar to cool slightly.

Strain the cooled vinegar through a sieve lined with cheesecloth or a clean thin cotton cloth, pouring slowly to catch any tomato pulp suspended in the vinegar.

Divide the tarragon stems among the sterilized bottles. Pour the cooled vinegar over the tarragon and fill each bottle, leaving ⅛-inch headspace. Seal the bottles, adjust the lids, and sterilize in a hot water bath for 10 minutes according to the instructions on page 135. Store in a cool, dry place.

Makes 4 pints

THIS OIL IS SUPERB for sautéing fish or chicken as it imparts a very subtle craw-fish flavor. Note that one of the steps below calls for chopping the crawfish while they are still alive. Unfortunately, there is no easy way to add the crawfish to the hot oil. Either you must kill them by adding them whole to the oil, which can cause the oil to splatter and can be extremely dangerous to the cook, or you can chop them up live. I prefer the chopping method to the boiling oil for my own safety.

When making flavored oils, make sure the sterilized jars are perfectly dry before adding the oil. If they are damp, the oil will become cloudy.

> *2 pounds live crawfish*
> *1 cup salt*
> *2 quarts canola or peanut oil*
> *1 fresh jalapeño pepper, stemmed and chopped, seeds remaining*

Sterilize four 1-pint jars and their lids according to the directions on page 134 and leave in the hot water.

Place the crawfish in a large, heavy pot and cover with fresh water. Add the salt to the pot and stir with a long-handled spoon. Allow to sit for 20 minutes to purge the crawfish of mud and impurities. Drain, then rinse under cold running water for 5 minutes. Drain and place the crawfish on a large chopping board and roughly chop into pieces. Set aside.

Heat the oil in a large, heavy pot over medium-high heat until it reaches 220°F on a candy thermometer. Add the chopped pepper and crawfish to the oil and heat to 220°F. Cook over a low flame until the oil clarifies, about 1 hour, stirring occasionally. Remove the pot from the heat and allow to cool.

Strain the oil through a sieve lined with cheesecloth or a clean thin cotton cloth. Do not force the oil through the cloth, but allow gravity to do the work. (This may take up to 1 hour.) When the oil has finished draining, pour it into a clean, heavy pot, discarding the crawfish and chopped pepper. Heat the oil over medium-high heat until it reaches 220°F and cook until it clarifies, about 10 minutes. (If the oil still appears cloudy after this step, strain it again through a clean cloth and reheat to 220°F for 10 minutes.)

Strain the oil through a sieve lined with clean cheesecloth into a large bowl. Allow the oil to cool. Pour the oil into the hot sterilized jars, adjust the lids, and store in a cool, dry place.

Makes 4 pints

BASIL PESTO OIL

DRIZZLE THIS ELIXIR over sun-warmed Louisiana Creole tomatoes or over fresh mozzarella cheese for a delightful summer lunch. While it might take considerable time for the pesto oil to drip through the cheesecloth, it is well worth the wait for the flavor of the finished product. Use the reserved pesto in other dishes, such as cooked pasta. Alternatively, spread it on bread, sprinkle with grated cheese, and lightly toast for an unusual dinner accompaniment.

> 2 cups fresh basil leaves, washed
> 1 cup toasted pine nuts
> 1 cup freshly grated Parmesan cheese
> 1 cup freshly grated Romano cheese
> 12 cloves garlic, peeled
> 10 crushed black peppercorns
> 4 cups pure olive oil

Sterilize two 1-pint jars and their lids according to the directions on page 134. Dry well and set aside. (If the jars are not completely dry when the oil is added, the oil will turn cloudy.)

Combine all of the ingredients except the olive oil in a food processor. Purée the mixture on high speed for 4 minutes. Add 1 cup of the olive oil and blend again on high speed for 1 minute. Remove the pesto from the processor and place in a mixing bowl. Stir in the remaining oil and mix thoroughly. Cover the bowl with plastic wrap and allow to sit overnight at room temperature.

Line a sieve with a double thickness of cheesecloth. Pour the pesto oil through the cloth into a bowl, allowing it to drip naturally; it will take about 2 to 3 hours. Remove the remaining basil pesto from the cloth, place in a jar, and refrigerate for later use. Pour the flavored oil into the sterilized jars, adjust the lids, and store in a cool, dry place.

Makes 2 pints

THIS IS A SENSATIONAL DRESSING for mixed greens or fresh spinach and can only be made in the summer when fresh tomatoes are at their peak. Just accompany your salad with warm French bread and you have the perfect light summer meal. This would also make a good dip or topping for grilled foods. It will keep in sealed jars in the refrigerator for 1 week.

¼ cup pure olive oil
¼ cup Champagne or malt vinegar
½ teaspoon fresh lemon juice
½ cup finely diced green tomatoes
½ cup finely diced red tomatoes
½ cup finely diced yellow tomatoes
¼ cup finely diced yellow onion
2 cloves garlic, peeled and minced
3 tablespoons chopped fresh cilantro
2 teaspoons finely chopped Italian parsley
Pinch ground cumin
Pinch ground coriander
Pinch powdered lemon peel
Pinch cayenne pepper
Salt to taste
Freshly ground black pepper to taste

Combine all of the ingredients in a large bowl and allow to stand for 1 to 2 hours at room temperature. Toss with mixed greens and serve.

Makes 2 pints

LEMON OIL

USE THIS AS A BASE for vinaigrette dressings or as an aromatic medium for cooking fish and shellfish. Lemon Oil is also terrific over freshly cooked pasta with just a sprinkling of chopped basil and freshly grated Parmesan cheese.

6 large lemons, washed
6 cloves
10 cups pure olive oil

Push 1 clove into the pulp of each lemon. Place the lemons in a large mixing bowl or stockpot. Add the olive oil to the bowl and cover with plastic wrap. Place the container in a cool, dry place for 2 months.

Sterilize five 1-pint jars and their lids or decorative bottles according to the directions on page 134. Dry well and set aside. (If the jars are not completely dry when the oil is added, the oil will turn cloudy.)

Remove the lemons from the oil and discard. Bottle the oil in the sterilized jars and store at room temperature.

Makes 5 pints

Using Three Tomato Salad Dressing

THESE SWEET POTATO CHIPS are delicious unadorned and are even better when served with Three Tomato Salad Dressing (page 99) for a dip. For a tricolor snack, make your own beet and regular potato chips (following the same recipe below) and serve with the sweet potato chips. Sweet potatoes are sometimes confused with yams but the sweet potato grows on a creeping vine, whereas the yam is a root vegetable. The confusion seems to be well accepted, as sweet potatoes are more often referred to as yams and are most popular when appearing as the holiday dish "candied yams." Sweet potatoes and yams can be used interchangeably in this recipe.

> 2 pounds sweet potatoes, washed and peeled
> 1 quart canola oil
> 2 teaspoons salt
> 1 teaspoon powdered sugar
> ½ teaspoon paprika
> ¼ teaspoon cayenne pepper

Cut the sweet potatoes into rounds 1/16-inch thick. Place the potato slices in a colander and rinse under cold running water for 5 minutes to remove the starchy residue. Dry the slices on kitchen towels.

Combine the salt, sugar, paprika, and cayenne pepper in a small bowl and set aside.

Place the oil in a large, heavy stockpot or large cast-iron skillet and place over medium-high heat. Heat the oil to 375°F. Cook the potatoes in the hot oil, a handful at a time, until crisp, about 4 minutes, occasionally stirring the slices with a long-handled spoon to keep them from sticking together.

Remove the chips from the oil and drain on paper towels. While the chips are still warm, sprinkle with the spice mixture. Repeat with the remaining potato slices. Serve immediately or store at room temperature in airtight containers lined with paper towels for up to 2 weeks.

Makes 1½ pounds

PICKLES
& relishes

WITH THEIR SHARP FLAVOR and tangy brininess, Creole Olives are quite addictive. Try them in the Olive Salad, opposite, or, for a spicy Louisiana-style salade niçoise, dice these olives and mix with pieces of freshly grilled tuna, steamed green beans, chopped fresh tomatoes, anchovy fillets, and a splash of olive oil. Any type of flaky fish, such as grouper or cod, can replace the tuna.

> *1 gallon whole green olives, packed in brine*
> *6 fresh jalapeño peppers, stems removed*
> *1 large yellow onion, peeled and finely shredded*
> *10 cloves garlic, peeled and crushed*
> *Zest of 2 lemons*

Drain the olives in a colander, reserving the brine. Cut the jalapeño peppers into ⅛-inch round slices. Combine the olives, jalapeño slices, onion, garlic, and lemon zest in the jar the olives were packed in. Pour the reserved brine into the jar and seal. Allow to sit in a cool, dry place for 2 weeks.

Serve the olives as an hors d'oeuvre or in Martini cocktails. Refrigerate after opening.

Makes 1 gallon

preceding pages: Pickled Watermelon Rind

OLIVE SALAD IS MOST COMMONLY SEEN in New Orleans on the Muffuletta, a mighty sandwich of Italian origins that even the Earl of Sandwich would have a hard time getting a grip on. The Muffuletta is made on a large round Italian loaf and is filled with thin slices of Genoa salami, baked ham, mortadella, and Swiss or Provolone cheeses. Olive Salad and often additional sliced peppers are added to the top of the meats and cheeses for a delicious, runny treat that can be served either hot or cold. The next time you are in New Orleans, treat yourself to a sandwich at its birthplace in the French Quarter, the Progress Grocery on Decatur Street.

Olive Salad is also delicious tossed with cold pastas and served as a topping to salads, pizzas, or other sandwiches. I think you'll find it difficult not to eat all of this salad in one sitting, although it will keep indefinitely in the refrigerator.

2 cups Creole Olives (opposite) or green olives, pitted
2 cups mixed pickled vegetables (cauliflower, carrots, celery), drained
¼ cup pickled sweet peppers
¼ cup finely chopped celery
¼ cup chopped parsley
2 tablespoons capers
2 teaspoons finely minced garlic
1 teaspoon dried oregano
2 tablespoons white wine vinegar
½ cup extra-virgin olive oil

Combine all of the ingredients in a large mixing bowl. Use immediately or spoon into a jar and refrigerate for later use.

Makes 5 cups

THIS IS MY FAVORITE RELISH. The sweetness of the corn really comes through and blends with whatever you pair with it, be it hot or cold. Try serving this relish with fried chicken, grilled fish, or even cheese and fresh bread.

10 cups fresh corn kernels (approximately 12 ears of corn)
2 cups shredded white cabbage
⅔ cup finely chopped yellow onion
⅔ cup finely chopped green bell pepper
⅔ cup finely chopped red bell pepper
½ cup granulated sugar
1 tablespoon Ground Mustard Seeds (page 55)
1½ teaspoons toasted mustard seeds (page 55)
1½ teaspoons celery seeds
1½ teaspoons ground turmeric
1 bay leaf
1 cup white wine vinegar

Sterilize six 1-pint jars and their lids according to the directions on page 134 and leave in the hot water.

Place 2 quarts salted water in a large, heavy pot. Bring to a boil over high heat. Add the corn kernels to the water, cover, and return to a boil. Remove the pot from the heat and allow it to stand, covered, for 5 minutes. Drain the corn, then return to the pot with the remaining ingredients and ¼ cup water. Bring to a boil over high heat, then reduce the heat and simmer, uncovered, for 20 minutes, stirring occasionally.

Remove the pot from the heat. Carefully pack the hot corn relish into the hot sterilized jars, leaving ⅛-inch headspace. Adjust the caps and seal. Allow to sit for 2 weeks before serving. Refrigerate after opening.

Makes 6 pints

THIS IS A DELIGHTFUL ACCOMPANIMENT to cold meat, fried chicken, and grilled ham. Open up a jar of Green Tomato Relish on a dreary winter's day—taste a bit of summer—and you'll be glad you made the effort to make it back in August. If green tomatoes are unavailable, use ripe, red tomatoes, but cook for up to 3 hours.

12 large green tomatoes, peeled, cored, and finely diced
3 tablespoons salt
3 green bell peppers, cored, seeded, and finely diced
3 red bell peppers, cored, seeded, and finely diced
6 medium yellow onions, peeled and finely diced
2 cups apple cider vinegar or malt vinegar
2 cups granulated sugar
½ teaspoon ground cinnamon
½ teaspoon celery seed
½ teaspoon ground allspice
¼ teaspoon red pepper flakes

Place a large colander in the sink. Place the tomatoes in the colander and sprinkle with the salt, stirring to coat evenly. Allow the tomatoes to sit and drain off excess liquid, about 1 hour.

Sterilize four 1-pint jars and their lids according to the instructions on page 134 and leave in the hot water.

Place 1 quart water in a large, heavy pot and bring to a rolling boil over high heat. Add the green and red bell peppers and onions to the water. Return to a boil over high heat and cook for 2 minutes. Drain the onions and peppers into a sieve and discard the cooking water. Return the onions and peppers to the pot. Add the tomatoes and remaining ingredients to the pot. Bring the mixture to a simmer over medium-high heat and cook, uncovered, until thickened, about 1½ hours, stirring from time to time.

Remove the pot from the heat and adjust seasoning to taste. Spoon the boiling hot relish into the hot sterilized jars, leaving ⅛-inch headspace. Adjust the caps and seal. Store the jars in a cool, dry place and allow the relish to sit for 1 month before using. Refrigerate after opening.

Makes 4 pints

THIS IS LIKE MARMALADE in consistency and makes an unusual accompaniment to any barbecued food. Or try serving the pickled rind with cold meats or cheeses. When preparing the rind for this recipe, cut away all the red meat and leave the white inner flesh attached to the striped rind.

> *2 pounds watermelon rind, cut into 1-inch-by-1¼-inch pieces*
> *1 tablespoon salt*
> *1 cup red wine vinegar*
> *1 vanilla pod, split open*
> *1½ cups granulated sugar*
> *½ teaspoon ground allspice*
> *½ teaspoon red pepper flakes*

Sterilize six 1-pint jars and their lids according to the directions on page 134 and leave in the hot water.

Place the watermelon and salt in a large, heavy stockpot. Bring to a boil over high heat and cook for 3 minutes. Pour the rind into a strainer and allow to drain for 20 minutes. Dry the rind between kitchen towels.

Combine the vinegar, vanilla pod, sugar, allspice, and red pepper flakes in a large, heavy saucepan. Bring to a boil over high heat and cook until the mixture thickens into a syrup, about 10 to 15 minutes. Add the watermelon rind to the pot and return to a boil over high heat. Cook until the rind is tender and easily pierced with a fork, about 2 minutes.

Remove from the heat and spoon the hot watermelon rind and liquid into the hot, sterilized jars, leaving ¼-inch headspace. Seal the jars and sterilize in a water bath for 20 minutes at 180°–185°F. according to the instructions on page 135. Store the jars in a cool, dry place and allow the pickles to sit for 2 to 3 weeks before eating. Refrigerate after opening.

Makes 6 pints

I LOVE THE SHARP BITE OF PICKLED JALAPEÑOS and the way they enhance the flavor of other foods. Try them thinly sliced and sprinkled on salads or as a garnish in soups. Jalapeños are downright hot but are still quite addictive, especially when accompanied by ice-cold beer on a hot summer's day.

When handling the peppers, wear rubber gloves in order to prevent burning the skin on your hands. If you don't wear gloves, be especially careful not to touch your eyes, nose, or mouth without first washing your hands well.

4 pounds fresh, unblemished jalapeño peppers, washed
8 cloves
6 cups apple cider vinegar or malt vinegar
¾ cup salt
¼ cup granulated sugar

With a small, sharp knife, cut a small slit at the pointed end of each pepper. Set aside.

Sterilize eight 1-pint jars and their lids according to the instructions on page 134. While the jars are still hot, pack each one tightly with the jalapeños, pointed side down, leaving ½-inch headspace at the top of each jar. Place 1 clove in each jar, then set the jars aside.

Combine the vinegar, salt, sugar, and 1½ cups water in a large, heavy saucepan. Bring the mixture to a boil over high heat. Reduce the heat to a simmer and cook until the sugar is dissolved, about 5 minutes, stirring from time to time.

Remove the pan from the heat. Pour the hot pickling liquid over the peppers, leaving ½-inch headspace at the top of each jar. Place the lids and bands on the jars and sterilize in a water bath according to the instructions on page 135 for 10 minutes at 180°–185° F.

Store the jars in a cool, dry place and allow to sit for 3 weeks before using. Refrigerate after opening.

Makes 8 pints

PICKLED Okra

IT IS SAID THAT OKRA was brought to the southern United States from West Africa by slaves who carried the seeds in their hair. In fact, the word "gumbo" is both an African word meaning okra and the name of the quintessential Louisiana soup that counts okra as one of its main ingredients. Okra is popular throughout the South and is most often stewed with tomatoes. It is also delicious cut into pieces, fried, and served with a creamy dipping sauce. Pickled okra makes a crunchy snack and, like Pickled Green Beans (page 115), is a great addition to Bloody Marys and Martinis.

If you like spicy foods, add more red pepper flakes to your Pickled Okra or even try adding a teaspoon (or more) of Seafood Boil Mix (page 27) to each jar.

2 pounds small, unbruised okra pods
1 tablespoon red pepper flakes
4 cloves garlic, peeled
4 medium bay leaves
2 teaspoons pickling spice
1 teaspoon mustard seeds
2 cups malt vinegar or cider vinegar
¼ cup pickling salt
1 tablespoon granulated sugar

Sterilize four 1-pint jars and their lids according to the directions on page 134 and leave in the hot water.

Wash and drain the okra. Trim the okra stems, leaving ½-inch of stem remaining. Pack the okra into the sterilized jars, pointed ends down, leaving 1-inch headspace. Into each jar add ½ teaspoon red pepper flakes, 1 garlic clove, 1 bay leaf, ½ teaspoon pickling spice, and ¼ teaspoon mustard seeds.

Combine 2 cups water, the vinegar, pickling salt, and sugar in a heavy saucepan. Bring the mixture to a boil over high heat. Reduce the heat and simmer for 2 minutes, stirring occasionally. Remove the pan from the heat and pour the hot liquid over the okra in each jar, leaving ½-inch of headspace in the jars. Seal the jars and sterilize in a water bath according to the directions on page 135 for 10 minutes at 180°–185°F. Store the jars in a cool, dry place and allow the pickles to sit for 4 weeks before eating. Refrigerate after opening.

Makes 4 pints

THESE SLICED PICKLES ARE A DELICIOUS addition to sandwiches, particularly leftover Thanksgiving turkey sandwiches, which always seem to need a lift. Or serve your Bread & Butter Pickles with all manner of picnic food, including sliced ham, pâté, and Hog's Head Cheese (page 116).

When making these pickles, be sure not to overcook them, as they should be firm, solid, and evenly colored. To achieve the wavy shape normally associated with this pickle, simply use a wavy cutter.

> *12 small to medium cucumbers, sliced into ⅛-inch rounds*
> *6 yellow onions, peeled and thinly sliced*
> *1 red bell pepper, cored, seeded, and finely diced*
> *1 cup kosher salt*
> *2½ cups apple cider vinegar*
> *2 cups granulated sugar*
> *2 teaspoons mustard seeds*
> *2 teaspoons ground turmeric*
> *2 teaspoons celery seeds*
> *¼ teaspoon ground cloves*
> *2 cloves garlic, peeled and minced*

Combine the cucumber slices, onions, bell pepper, and salt in a large mixing bowl and stir to combine well. Pour ice water into the bowl to cover the ingredients and allow to stand for 3 hours. Place the mixture in a colander and allow to drain for 1 hour, tossing occasionally.

Meanwhile, sterilize four 1-pint jars and their lids according to the directions on page 134 and leave in the hot water.

Combine the remaining ingredients in a large, heavy saucepan. Bring the mixture to a boil over high heat and add the cucumber mixture to the pan. Return the mixture to a boil, lower the heat, and simmer for 10 minutes.

Pour the hot pickles directly into the hot, sterilized jars, leaving ⅛-inch headspace. Adjust the caps. Sterilize the jars in a hot water bath at 180°–185°F. for 10 minutes according to the instructions on page 135. Allow to sit in a cool, dark place for 3 months before serving. Refrigerate after opening.

Makes 4 pints

THESE GREEN BEANS make great edible stirrers in Martinis and Bloody Marys, and are also good to have on hand for easy party finger food.

3 pounds large, fresh green beans, washed
5 teaspoons fennel seeds
10 cloves garlic, peeled
2 tablespoons black peppercorns
5 teaspoons red pepper flakes
5 medium bay leaves
5 teaspoons pickling spice
¼ cup pickling salt
3 cups malt vinegar

Sterilize five 1-pint jars and their lids according to the directions on page 134 and leave in the hot water.

Evenly trim the green beans so that when placed straight up in the 1-pint jars there will be ½-inch headspace at the top. Set aside.

Place 2 quarts water in a large, heavy stockpot and bring to a boil over high heat. Add the trimmed beans to the water and blanch for 3 minutes. Remove the beans from the pot and drain in a colander. Place the beans in ice water for 5 minutes to set their color. Dry the beans on kitchen towels and set aside.

Into each sterilized jar place 1 teaspoon fennel seeds, 2 cloves garlic, 10 black peppercorns, 1 teaspoon red pepper flakes, 1 bay leaf, and 1 teaspoon pickling spice. Pack the green beans tightly into the jars, leaving ½-inch headspace.

Combine 3 cups water, the pickling salt, and vinegar in a small, heavy saucepan and bring to a boil over high heat. Lower the heat and simmer for 5 minutes, stirring from time to time. Remove from the heat and pour over the green beans, leaving ½-inch headspace in the jars. Sterilize the jars in a hot water bath according to the instructions on page 135 and process for 10 minutes at 180°–185°F. Store the jars in a cool, dry place and allow the beans to sit for 1 month before using. Refrigerate after opening.

Makes 5 pints

HOG'S HEAD cheese

ORIGINALLY THIS RECIPE CALLED FOR a whole hog's head, hog's feet, and cow knee bones, all of which might be hard to find today at your local supermarket—unless you're in Louisiana, where a request of this sort won't even turn the local butcher's head. To make your shopping easier and the cooking process a good bit more palatable, I've made a few substitutions here for a more modern delicacy. Believe it or not, pig's feet are usually available no matter where you live, and in South Louisiana you always see Hog's Head Cheese in supermarket deli cases, along with pickled pig's feet and pickled pig's lips. If you prefer your Hog's Head Cheese to have a smoother consistency, after the final cooking, blend the meat and cooking liquid in a food processor until it has the texture of a fine purée, then pour it into the loaf pans and chill.

The method for making Hog's Head Cheese is essentially the same as that used for making *rillettes*—the French cook's economical way of using up pork or poultry scraps. In both recipes the meat is stewed down until it reaches a thick paste-like consistency and is then put away to gel before eating. Obviously, Creole Hog's Head Cheese came to the Louisiana table via the French *rillette*; in fact, in certain parts of Louisiana the meat is blended with its cooking liquid so it actually more closely resembles the *rillette*.

In Cheshire, England, where I come from, this dish is called brawn. I remember a neighbor, Samuel Hazeldine, making a delicious batch each Christmas season.

1½ pounds pork shoulder on the bone, skin removed
1 pig's foot
1 large yellow onion, peeled and finely chopped
5 cloves garlic, peeled and minced
½ cup chopped celery
½ cup chopped scallions
2 tablespoons champagne vinegar or white wine vinegar
1 tablespoon powdered gelatin
1 medium bay leaf

½ teaspoon cayenne pepper
½ teaspoon Creole Herbs (page 22)
Dash Worcestershire sauce
¼ teaspoon salt
¼ teaspoon freshly ground black pepper
Salted crackers, for serving
Bread and Butter Pickles (page 113) and/or Creole Mustard (page 57) or Dijon
    mustard, Pickled Okra (page 112), or Pickled Jalapeños (page 111), for serving

Place all of the ingredients through the black pepper in a large, heavy stockpot and cover with cold water. Place the pot over high heat and bring to a boil. Reduce the heat and simmer until the meat falls from the bone, about 2 hours, skimming the surface from time to time to remove any scum that may have risen to the top. Remove the pot from the heat and drain, reserving the liquid.

Remove the meat from the bones and set aside. Discard the bones. As the cooking liquid cools, strain off the fat that rises to the surface and discard. Return the meat, cooking liquid, and vegetables to the stockpot. Bring the mixture to a boil over high heat. Reduce the heat and simmer until it reaches the consistency of a thick stew, about 30 to 40 minutes. Remove the pot from the heat and allow to cool. Stir the mixture from time to time to prevent it from separating. Season with salt and pepper to taste.

Divide the Hog's Head Cheese among 2 (1-pound/2-cup) disposable aluminum loaf pans and refrigerate overnight or until well set. Remove a pan from the refrigerator and run a knife around the edge of the cheese to loosen, then dip in a hot water bath for 10 seconds. Invert the pan onto a serving dish. Repeat with remaining pan. Serve with salted crackers and Bread and Butter Pickles and/or Creole Mustard, Pickled Okra, or Pickled Jalapeños. Store for up to 3 to 4 weeks in the refrigerator; do not freeze.

Makes 2 pounds

STOCKS
& basics

YOU MAY ASK, "Why such a simple recipe?" Because I think we've forgotten the true taste of butter, being accustomed as we are to the packaged variety, with its antioxidants, stabilizers, heavy salt, and such. Before the advent of prepackaged butter the Creoles, like everyone else, enjoyed creamery fresh butter that in many cases they (or their cooks) churned themselves. And with the buttermilk that came from the butter-making process, they made biscuits, pancakes, and other baked goods. As with most Creole recipes, there was no waste.

Instead of baking with the residual buttermilk, try cooking whole new potatoes or fresh carrots in it. The flavor of fresh vegetables cooked in this manner is unbelievably rich. Or make mashed potatoes or polenta with fresh buttermilk instead of butter.

The worst enemy of butter is light so be sure to wrap your homemade butter in aluminum foil to keep the light out. Homemade butter will keep in the refrigerator for 2 months or can be frozen for up to 6 months. Unlike store brands, which have only 2% milk fat, homemade buttermilk has a very high fat content. The buttermilk will keep up to 1 week refrigerated; stir before using. The small amount of salt in this recipe is not added for flavor but to help preserve the butter.

2 quarts heavy cream, at room temperature
Pinch salt

Place the cream in the bowl of an electric mixer and whip on low speed until the cream breaks down into butter. (You will see the light yellow granules of butter fat floating in the white buttermilk. The time this process takes depends on the temperature of the cream and the speed at which you whip it.)

Line a large bowl with a double layer of cheesecloth and pour the butter and buttermilk into it. Pull up the sides of the cheesecloth and knead it against the sides of the bowl to wring out as much buttermilk as possible from the cloth into the bowl. (There should be equal amounts of milk and solids.)

When the milk has been wrung from the solids, unwrap the cheesecloth and place on a clean work surface. Fold in the salt with a wooden spoon. With 2 wooden spoons or your hands, form the butter into 2 equal size bricks, then wrap tightly in aluminum foil. Pour the buttermilk into an airtight container. Refrigerate the butter and buttermilk until ready to use.

Makes 2 pounds butter and 1 quart buttermilk

Using Homemade Sweet Butter

THESE BISCUITS ARE QUITE RICH, as they are made with heavy cream rather than the usual buttermilk and include eggs and pecans. The resulting flavor and texture are cake-like and sweeter than the usual biscuits. If pecans are unavailable, try walnuts. Serve these for breakfast with Homemade Sweet Butter (opposite) or Pontchatoula Strawberry Jam (page 46), or as a filling afternoon snack with coffee or iced tea.

To make the traditional Southern brunch favorite, omit the pecans from this recipe, split the biscuits in half, and fill with a slice of smoked ham. Serve with eggs or grits.

> *4 cups all-purpose flour*
> *¼ cup granulated sugar*
> *1 tablespoon baking powder*
> *1½ teaspoons salt*
> *¾ cup cold **Homemade Sweet Butter** (opposite)*
> *   or unsalted butter, finely chopped*
> *1½ cups heavy cream*
> *4 large eggs*
> *½ cup chopped pecans*

Combine the flour, sugar, baking powder, salt, and butter in a large mixing bowl. Using an electric mixer on low speed, beat the mixture until it resembles a coarse meal. Add the cream and eggs and mix until blended. The dough will be slightly sticky. Fold in the pecan pieces, cover with plastic wrap, and refrigerate for 1 hour.

Preheat the oven to 450°F.

Line a baking sheet with greased parchment or waxed paper. On a lightly floured surface, knead the dough gently for 1 minute, adding more flour as necessary to achieve a smooth consistency. Pat or roll the dough to a thickness of ¾ inch. Cut the dough into rounds with a 2-inch biscuit cutter and place on the prepared baking sheet.

Place the baking sheet in the preheated oven and bake for about 12 to 15 minutes, or until golden brown.

Serve hot with butter, jam, or jelly.

Makes about 3 dozen

Using Homemade Sweet Butter & Vanilla Sugar

IN THE TRADITIONAL FRENCH KITCHEN "praline" means sugared. According to legend, sugar-coated almonds got the name pralines from the Marachel de Plessin Pralin who loved almonds but could not eat them because they gave him indigestion. His butler advised him to eat them sugar-coated to ease his discomfort, and hence a culinary treat was born. In New Orleans, the treat evolved into a type of brittle made with nuts and caramelized sugar.

Pralines are a delicious accompaniment to ice cream or on their own with after-dinner coffee. For an interesting variation, try this recipe with almonds, peanuts, or filberts instead of pecans.

1 stick (½ cup) Homemade Sweet Butter (page 120) or
    unsalted butter
1 cup heavy cream
2¼ cups packed dark brown sugar
2 cups Vanilla Sugar (page 38) or granulated sugar
2 cups pecan pieces, roughly chopped

Line 2 large baking sheets with waxed paper.

In a heavy saucepan, combine the butter, cream, and sugars. Bring to a boil over high heat and stir in the pecans. Return to a boil, stir, then remove from the heat.

Drop the mixture from a soup spoon onto the waxed paper to make 1½-inch circles. Work quickly as the mixture will crystallize rapidly. Allow the pralines to harden at room temperature for 6 hours.

Carefully peel the pralines from the waxed paper and store in airtight containers at room temperature for up to 2 weeks.

Makes approximately 5 dozen

MAYONNAISE IS PRONOUNCED "MY-ON-AYSE" in New Orleans, where it is a favorite addition to many cold summer suppers and salads. It is also an integral component of the Po' Boy (a sandwich made with thickly sliced French bread, deep-fried seafood or roast beef, gravy, and cheese), which when ordered "dressed" comes to the table with a thick slather of mayonnaise, lettuce, and tomatoes.

The mayonnaise we use today is a pale shadow of the rich sauce of the past. The only problem is that it is a true emulsion and, therefore, will break if refrigerated. Yet it is worth making, even in the smallest quantity, as the flavor wraps itself around the food it accompanies rather than masks it.

If you must, this mayonnaise will keep for up to 4 days in the refrigerator, although I suggest eating it right away. To reconstitute after refrigeration, simply beat the sauce back together.

> *2 large egg yolks*
> *2 teaspoons malt vinegar*
> *⅛ teaspoon ground mustard seeds (page 55)*
> *Dash Worcestershire Sauce*
> *Pinch salt*
> *Pinch white pepper*
> *1 cup pure olive oil*

Bring all of the ingredients to room temperature. Combine the egg yolks, vinegar, mustard, Worcestershire, salt, and pepper in a bowl and mix well with a wire whisk. Slowly add the olive oil to the bowl in a thin, steady stream, beating constantly with the whisk to form an emulsion. Keep beating until all the oil has been added. Adjust the seasoning to taste. Serve.

Makes 1½ cups

THERE'S AN INSIDE JOKE AMONG LOUISIANA COOKS when relating Creole recipes. One cook says to the other, "First you make a roux . . ." and everyone within earshot laughs, knowing that nearly every Creole recipe begins in this manner. Straight from traditional French cooking, the French Creoles brought roux to the Louisiana kitchen to thicken their new cuisine. If roux are cooked a short time, just long enough to form a thick base, they are a light blond color and impart a subtle, slight taste; if cooked longer, up to 45 minutes, and a heavy fat (such as bacon grease) is used, they can be a dark walnut color, or almost black, and can impart a dark, smoky flavor into a dish.

The fatless roux recipe presented here is different from traditional roux recipes in that unhealthy fats or oils have been eliminated. Fatless Roux will keep indefinitely in a sealed container in the refrigerator or freezer. Be careful when making this recipe, as the roux will become very hot in the oven.

To use Fatless Roux in other recipes, combine ¼ cup of prepared roux for each ½ cup liquid and stir well to form a paste. Slowly pour the roux paste into gently boiling liquid, stirring constantly. If the color of the thickened liquid is not dark enough, add a bit of Blackjack (page 127) as a coloring agent.

4 cups all-purpose flour

Preheat the oven to 375°F.

Place the flour in a heavy roasting pan and place in the oven. When the flour begins to brown on the surface, after about 25 minutes, open the oven and stir with a long-handled wooden spoon, breaking up any lumps that have formed. Continue to stir the flour every 5 minutes until it reaches a nut brown color, about 1 hour. (As the flour reaches this stage, it will begin to smell like hazelnuts.) Remove the roux from the oven and let it cool. When cool enough to handle, strain the roux through a sieve to remove any lumps. Add the warm roux immediately to any dish as a thickening agent or store in an airtight container in the refrigerator until ready to use.

Makes 4 cups

FOR THOSE WHO WANT TO MAKE ROUX the "old-fashioned way," fat and all, here's a traditional roux recipe. The secret to making this is to do it at your own speed, watching and stirring all the while, until the roux takes on the desired color, although this may take up to an hour. Note that this roux must be stirred continuously to avoid scorching and burning along the bottom of the pan. If the roux is cooked too quickly it will turn bitter and add a bitterness to your completed dish. As with the Fatless Roux (page 125), this roux will keep indefinitely in an airtight container in the refrigerator.

> *2 cups vegetable oil*
> *2 cups all-purpose flour*

Place the vegetable oil in a large, heavy saucepan over medium heat. Add the flour to the pan and lower the heat to a simmer, stirring constantly to incorporate the flour into the hot oil. Cook the roux slowly, stirring constantly, until it begins to smell like roasted nuts and takes on the desired color.

Remove the pan from the heat and allow to cool. Immediately add the warm roux to any dish as a thickening agent or store indefinitely in an airtight container in the refrigerator.

Makes 4 cups

BLACKJACK IS A HANDY, FLAVORLESS ingredient used in professional kitchens to add caramel coloring to foods. Add it to Fatless Roux (page 125), soups, or anything else you would like to color slightly.

4 cups granulated sugar

Place the sugar in a heavy saucepan over low heat. Stir the sugar constantly and simmer until it goes through all the stages (from soft boil to caramelization) and begins to blacken, about 20 minutes. Remove the pan from the heat and add 2 cups water to the pan all at once, being very careful not to burn yourself. Once the sugar has stopped bubbling and popping, stir well.

Return the pan to low heat and cook slowly until the burnt sugar dissolves, about 4 to 5 minutes. Remove the pan from the heat and allow to cool. Bottle and use for coloring soups, stews, and sauces.

Makes 2 cups

SEAFOOD gumbo

THERE ARE AS many gumbo recipes as there are kitchens in Louisiana. Let this recipe serve as your jumping-off point—the seasonings and roux are really just your base. Substitute fish, chicken, or sausage for the shrimp and crawfish, and you'll have an entirely different dish.

2 quarts homemade Chicken Stock (page 132)
   or canned reduced-sodium chicken broth
1 tablespoon peanut oil
1 large yellow onion, peeled and diced
1 large tomato, peeled, cored, and diced
½ cup finely diced red bell pepper
½ cup finely diced green bell pepper
½ cup chopped celery
5 cloves garlic, peeled and crushed
2 medium bay leaves
Pinch dried thyme
Pinch dried oregano
1 cup cooked crawfish tails
1 cup raw shrimp
1 teaspoon Creole Seasoning (page 18)
Pinch cayenne pepper
½ cup Fatless Roux (page 125)
Rice, for serving (page 53)
Hot Pepper Sauce, for serving (page 50)

Place the chicken stock in a large saucepan and bring to a simmer over medium heat. Cover the pot, remove from the heat, and keep warm.

In a large, heavy stockpot, heat the peanut oil over medium heat. Add the onion, tomato, red and green bell peppers, celery, garlic, bay leaves, thyme, and oregano and sauté, stirring constantly, until the vegetables lose half their volume, about 20 minutes.

Add the crawfish tails, shrimp, Creole Seasoning, and cayenne pepper to the vegetables and cook for an additional 5 minutes, stirring constantly. Gradually stir in the precooked Fatless Roux, 1 tablespoon at a time, stirring constantly. (The mixture will thicken as the roux is added.)

Slowly add the warm stock to the pot, ½ cup at a time, stirring well to incorporate. Adjust the seasoning to taste. Lower the heat and simmer the gumbo for 30 to 40 minutes, stirring from time to time. Serve immediately over hot rice, passing Hot Pepper Sauce at the table.

Makes 3 quarts

GLACE DE VIANDE IS a highly concentrated beef stock. Glace has a longer shelf life than a stock made in the usual fashion—it will keep indefinitely in an airtight container in the refrigerator—and it won't turn sour like a regular beef stock.

Glace de Viande makes a delicious hot or cold consommé. Simply add 1 tablespoon Glace de Viande to 2 cups hot water, stirring well to incorporate. To make a rich homemade gravy, stir 1 teaspoon Glace de Viande into the pan drippings from a roast, or for a wholesome snack, simply spread the warm Glace de Viande on toast.

3 pounds ground shin beef
2 pig's feet or 1 cow's knuckle (optional)
2 large onions, peeled and finely chopped
2 large tomatoes, crushed
1 large carrot, finely diced
6 stalks celery, finely diced
6 cloves garlic, peeled and minced
1 teaspoon Creole Herbs (page 22)
2 cups red wine

Place the ground meat, pig's feet, and 1 cup water in a large, heavy stockpot. Bring to a boil over high heat, cover, and cook until the meat is brown, about 25 minutes. (The steam breaks down and renders the fat in the meat, and it is this fat that, in turn, browns the meat.)

Add the onions, tomatoes, carrot, celery, garlic, and Creole Herbs to the pot. Cook over medium heat until all the vegetables are cooked down, about 25 minutes, stirring from time to time. Add the wine and 2 gallons water to the pot and return to a boil over high heat. Reduce the heat to low and simmer the mixture, uncovered, for 3 hours, skimming the surface from time to time to remove any scum that may have formed.

Remove the pot from the heat and strain the stock into a clean, large saucepan. Place the pan over medium-low heat and reduce by half, to about 1 quart of liquid; this will take about 1 hour. Remove the pan from the heat. To test if the Glace de Viande is ready, dip a spoon into the pan and allow to cool slightly. If finished, the Glace will feel sticky and won't separate; rather, it will pull into threads between your fingers.

Strain through a fine strainer and allow to cool. Place the Glace de Viande in clean jars and refrigerate until ready to use.

Makes 1 quart

BECAUSE COLD-WATER FISH ARE MUCH LESS OILY than warm-water fish, their bones are far less likely to cloud the stock. If desired, vary the taste or color of this stock by adding such ingredients as tomato skins, saffron, or fresh herbs.

¼ cup vegetable oil
4 pounds cold-water fish bones (such as sole, turbot, halibut or whiting), thoroughly washed and cut to a manageable size)
2 medium yellow onions, peeled and roughly chopped
1 small bunch celery, washed and roughly chopped
1 bunch parsley, chopped
2 large leeks, white parts only, washed and roughly chopped
8 cloves garlic, peeled and roughly chopped
2 medium bay leaves
1 sprig fresh thyme
2 cups dry white wine (optional)

Heat the oil in a large, heavy stock pot over medium-high heat. Add the fish bones, onions, celery, parsley, leeks, bay leaves, garlic, and thyme. Raise the heat to high and sauté, stirring constantly, until the onions become translucent. Remove the pot from the heat, cover, and let sit for 10 minutes.

Return the pot to high heat and add the wine (if using) and 1 gallon cold water. Bring to a boil, uncovered, skimming any foam that forms on the surface. Reduce the heat and simmer for 30 minutes.

Remove the pot from the heat and skim the surface a final time. Strain the stock into a clean container and cool to room temperature. Use right away or allow to cool completely and freeze in 1-cup portions for up to 3 months.

Makes 4 quarts

THIS STOCK MAY BE COVERED and stored in the refrigerator for 1 week or frozen in small portions for up to 3 months.

4 pounds chicken bones
2 white onions, peeled and roughly chopped
2 medium bay leaves
½ head celery, trimmed and roughly chopped
2 leeks, white parts only, thoroughly rinsed and roughly chopped
10 to 12 white peppercorns

Combine all of the ingredients in a large, heavy stockpot. Add 1 gallon water. Bring the mixture to a boil over high heat, skimming any scum that forms on the surface. Lower the heat and simmer, uncovered, for 1 hour, skimming any additional scum that forms on the surface.
    Strain and cool.

Makes 3 quarts

USE THIS RECIPE AS A LOOSE GUIDE for making vegetable stock. Depending on the flavor base you wish for your finished dish, choose other vegetables, such as turnips or bell peppers, in addition to, or to the exclusion of the other vegetables called for here. Or, for an even quicker stock base, use the water from boiling vegetables (such as potatoes or cabbage) then infuse it with whatever additional vegetables or herbs you wish. The wine can either be omitted using this technique or it can be added at the last minute (after the vegetables are removed).

> ¼ cup olive oil
> 2 large yellow onions, peeled and roughly chopped
> 1 large carrot, washed and roughly chopped
> 1 large leek, white part only, washed and roughly chopped
> ½ head white cabbage, washed and roughly chopped
> 6 stalks celery, washed and roughly chopped
> 8 cloves garlic, peeled and roughly chopped
> 2 medium bay leaves
> 1 sprig fresh thyme
> 1 teaspoon white peppercorns
> 1 cup dry white wine (optional)

Heat the oil in a large, heavy stockpot over medium-high heat. Add all of the remaining ingredients, stirring to mix well. Lower the heat, cover the pot, and cook very slowly until all the vegetables are soft, about 45 minutes, stirring occasionally. Add 1 gallon water to the pot and bring to a boil. Reduce the heat and simmer for 15 minutes. Remove the pot from the heat and strain into a clean container. Use right away or allow to cool completely and freeze in 1-cup portions for up to 3 months.

Makes 1 gallon

STERILIZING Jars

USE SPECIAL, COMMERCIALLY AVAILABLE CANNING JARS and lids with screw-on bands for the best results. Jars and lids not manufactured specifically for home-canning can lead to dangerous breakage and seal failure.

Assemble the jars called for in the recipe and make sure there are no nicks, cracks, or sharp edges; always use new lids. Wash the jars, screw-on bands, and lids required for the canning process in hot soapy water and rinse well.

Place the jars, right side up, on a rack or kitchen towel in a large stockpot and cover with hot, not boiling, water. Place the pot over high heat and bring to a steady boil for 10 minutes. Keep the jars hot until ready to use, saving the hot water for processing filled jars, as necessary.

THE BOILING WATER BATH utilized in home-canning processes foods at a temperature of 212°F., thereby destroying bacteria that can cause spoilage or poisoning in acid foods. This method is simple to undertake and can be achieved with basic kitchen tools. If you do not have a wire rack that fits into your stockpot for sterilizing the jars, simply place a thick piece of cardboard or a folded, clean kitchen towel on the bottom of the pot to keep the jars from rattling.

Prepare the food according to the recipe and pack into the sterilized jars (opposite), being sure to leave the specified headspace. (This space is essential for the expansion of food as it processes and forms a vacuum in the cooled jars.)

Remove the air bubbles in a filled jar by running a rubber spatula down the sides of the jar and lightly tapping the jar on the countertop to release air bubbles. Add more liquid, if necessary, to fill the jar to the required level. Wipe the top and threads of the jar with a clean, damp cloth. Put the lid on firmly and screw the band down evenly and tightly so that the rubber sealing compound is against the top of the jar.

As each jar is filled, carefully return it to the rack in the stockpot, placing jars 1 inch apart. The water in the pot should be hot, but not boiling. Add more water as needed so that there is at least 1 inch of water above the tops of the jars at all times. Cover the pot with a snug lid and bring the water to a full boil. Process for the length of time required in the recipe, timing from the moment the water actually returns to a steady, gentle boil.

Carefully remove the hot, processed jars from the pot with long-handled tongs. Place the jars right side up on a rack or work surface padded with a kitchen towel. Allow the jars to cool at room temperature for 12 hours. Remove the bands from the jars 12 hours after canning. If the center of the lid is down or stays down when pressed, the jar is properly sealed. (If the lids do not stay down, reprocess the food for the full length of time or refrigerate and use as soon as possible.) Store the jars in a dark, dry place without their bands until ready to use. After use, close the jars with both the lids and the bands.

BUTTER

Some confusion may arise over the measuring of butter and other hard fats. In the United States butter is generally sold in one-pound packages that contain four equal "sticks." The wrapper on each stick is marked to show tablespoons, so the cook can cut the stick according to the quantity required. The equivalent weights are:

1 stick = 115 g / 4 oz
1 tablespoon = 15 g / ½ oz

FLOUR

American all-purpose flour is milled from a mixture of hard and soft wheats, whereas British plain flour is made mainly from soft wheat. To achieve a near equivalent to American all-purpose flour, use half British plain flour and half strong bread flour.

SUGAR

In the recipes in this book, if sugar is called for it is to be granulated, unless otherwise specified. American granulated sugar is finer than British granulated, closer to caster sugar, so British cooks should use caster sugar throughout.

INGREDIENTS AND EQUIPMENT GLOSSARY

The following ingredients and equipment are basically the same on both sides of the Atlantic, but have different names.

AMERICAN	BRITISH
bell pepper	sweet pepper (capsicum)
biscuit	scone
broiler/to broil	grill/to grill
cheesecloth	muslin
red pepper flakes	dried crushed red chilli
heavy cream	whipping cream
(37.6% fat)	(35–40% fat)
hot pepper sauce	Tabasco sauce
jelly/jam	jam
kitchen towel	tea towel
parchment paper	nonstick baking paper
peanut oil	groundnut oil
Romano cheese	pecorino cheese
scallion	spring onion
shrimp	prawn (varying in size)
skillet	frying pan
tomato purée	sieved tomatoes
	or pasatta
whole milk	homogenized milk

OVEN TEMPERATURES

In the recipes given in this book, only Fahrenheit temperatures have been given. Consult this chart for the Centigrade and gas mark equivalents.

OVEN	°F	°C	GAS MARK
very cool	250–275	130–140	½–1
cool	300	150	2
warm	325	170	3
moderate	350	180	4
moderately hot	375	190	5
	400	200	6
hot	425	220	7
very hot	450	230	8
	475	250	9

VOLUME EQUIVALENTS

These are not exact equivalents for the American cups and spoons, but have been rounded up or down slightly to make measuring easier.

AMERICAN	METRIC	IMPERIAL
¼ t	1.25 ml	
½ t	2.5 ml	
1 t	5 ml	
½ T (1½ t)	7.5 ml	
1 T (3 t)	15 ml	
¼ cup (4 T)	60 ml	2 fl oz
⅓ cup (5 T)	75 ml	2½ fl oz
½ cup (8 T)	125 ml	4 fl oz
⅔ cup (10 T)	150 ml	5 fl oz (¼ pint)
¾ cup (12 T)	175 ml	6 fl oz
1 cup (16 T)	250 ml	8 fl oz
1¼ cups	300 ml	10 fl oz (½ pint)
1½ cups	350 ml	12 fl oz
1 pint (2 cups)	500 ml	16 fl oz
1 quart (4 cups)	1 litre	1¾ pints

WEIGHT EQUIVALENTS

The metric weights given in this chart are not exact equivalents, but have been rounded up or down slightly to make measuring easier.

AVOIRDUPOIS	METRIC
¼ oz	7 g
½ oz	15 g
1 oz	30 g
2 oz	60 g
3 oz	90 g
4 oz	115 g
5 oz	150 g
6 oz	175 g
7 oz	200 g
8 oz (½ lb)	225 g
9 oz	250 g
10 oz	300 g
11 oz	325 g
12 oz	350 g
13 oz	375 g
14 oz	400 g
15 oz	425 g
1 lb	450 g
1 lb 2 oz	500 g
1 ½ lb	750 g
2 lb	900 g
2 ¼ lb	1 kg
3 lb	1.4 kg
4 lb	1.8 kg
4 ½ lb	2 kg

ACKNOWLEDGMENTS

I WOULD LIKE TO THANK the following people who have helped make this book possible:

Leslie Stoker, my publisher, for her constant encouragement and guidance

Susi Oberhelman for her creative and beautiful design

Trevor Wisdom Lawrence, for her help with recipe testing and writing

Zeva Oelbaum, for her stunning photography

Melanie Falick, for her skillful editing and commitment to excellence

Susan Ehlich, for her elegant food styling

The Artisan team: Jim Wageman, Hope Koturo, Beth Wareham, Eliza Kunkel, NeelieWhite, and Ann ffolliott; and freelancers Cathy Dorsey, Susan Kirby, Siobhan McGowan, and Kerry Acker

INDEX

Page numbers in italic refer to illustrations.

Designed by
SUSI OBERHELMAN

Typefaces in this book are
Monotype Columbus and Celestia Antiqua

Printed and bound by
ARNOLDO MONDADORI EDITORE S.P.A. • VERONA, ITALY